Making a Difference

Beatrice Kiraso

authorHOUSE®

AuthorHouse™ UK Ltd.
500 Avebury Boulevard
Central Milton Keynes, MK9 2BE
www.authorhouse.co.uk
Phone: 08001974150

First published by AuthorHouse   6/23/2011

ISBN: 978-1-4567-7817-0 (sc)

To my beloved children, Eva and Joshua, who have over the years provided perfect companionship, a good reason to live and an opportunity for me to discover myself. Without them, life would have no doubt been different, but certainly not better. I love you.

18 April, 2005: I am lying on my bed in the Olympe Hotel, Bamako, Mali, having retired earlier than I had expected from the session of the African, Carribean, Pacific/European Union (ACP/EU) Joint Parliamentary Assembly. I have been here for six days now and each day I keep promising myself I will start this book. The idea of writing a book has been on my mind for quite some time—in fact, more than a year—but I have been either too lazy or too busy to begin putting the ideas together.

I had one big question whenever I thought of writing something: What should I write about? Politics? No, it now bores me to death. Love? I don't know much about the subject. Women? So much has already been written about how they are discriminated against and how their rights are violated, so I will not make much difference; Men? I risk my book not being read, because I doubt even they want to know more than they already do about themselves. That leaves a whole range of other issues, like cars, wars, drugs, weapons of mass destruction, macroeconomic stability, or even structural adjustment programs and economic reforms. But these would require me to do research, compile data and statistics as if I were writing a dissertation for my PhD.

So I decided to write about something I know without having to research it, something I know first-hand and no one else knows as much as I do, so that I can *make a difference.*

INTRODUCTION

I was born forty-four years ago to Ms Rose Mary Kabadaaki and Mr Edison Rusoke Kiraso at Virika Catholic Hospital in Fort Portal town, Kabarole District, in the Kingdom of Tooro. This is in the mid-west of Uganda, a short distance from the slopes of the spectacular, undulating Rwenzori Mountains.

My mother, fondly known to her friends and close family as Nyinabarongo (mother of twins), was a primary school teacher, now retired. I am her first born, followed by twins (both girls). She had me before she finished her teacher's training course, and she tells me I am the reason she did not finish, although I always tease her that she is actually the reason. Then she teasingly says my father is the reason. Anyway, whatever the reason is, she loves me—actually, she adores me—because I have endeavored to make a difference in her life.

My father is a civil engineer by profession, long retired from public service. He worked in his home district for most of his working life and he surely has something to show for it—a good home, dairy farms, and tea estates—and he is blessed with an understanding and loving wife and ten children. While my mother had seven other children and my father had nine, I am the first on either side.

My stepmother (I hate to call her that), is an extraordinary human being. One would have to be very nosy to discover that I am not her real first-born child. It is something that seldom arises. I am greatly indebted to her because she made such a difference in my life when I was growing up.

PART I

I come from a big family, both immediate and extended. It is big in size as well as influence. My grandfather was a subcounty chief during the reign of King George Rukidi III, and that meant a lot that time. He passed away on 9 February 1991, almost fifteen years ago, but the family still feels his presence as if he is away on a visit and will be back soon. He instilled in all of us who were old enough to know him so many values, including unconditional love, selflessness, kindness, and most important, respect for and fear of God. He analysed situations intellectually and placed people where he though they belonged, but he still accepted them the way they were.

We have honoured his non-discriminatory approach towards his many children, nephews, and nieces by remaining a close-knit family. I am particularly proud that my uncles and aunties and their children are my friends.

No two people are exactly the same. As we grow up, the best and the worst in us comes out, and therefore we relate to each other differently. This has been true for my siblings and me. Though there are no extremes to talk about here, we have over the years learnt to appreciate each other's strengths and to accommodate each other's weaknesses. On the whole, the differences between us have made a positive difference in our lives. This does not mean we have not hurt, angered, or fallen short of the expectations of others. Outside my family, I have interacted many different people, in many different situations.

Making a Difference is about what I know, what I have seen, learnt, loved, ignored, done, said, and thought, and the difference all that has made for me—at home, at school, at work, in politics, and with the different people that I have been blessed to interact with. They too have made a difference and assisted me to live a full life.

CHAPTER 1

'Go and wash quickly; put on your new dress. There are people in the car out at the road who have come to see you.' I do not remember exactly how old I was when my mum made this confusing statement to me one day around noon. I was probably three years old or so, and she completely confused me. But it was my mother talking to me, and she herself was going to walk down to the car with me. I could not figure out why my little twin sisters were not coming to the car with me to see 'the visitors'. Neither did I know why the 'visitors' were not coming to the house. It was not like now when children ask whys and how, so I kept quiet and just obliged. Not that it meant anything, but thinking back, and now knowing about rights, I think I should have been told who these people were, why they wanted to see me and not my sisters, and why in the car, not at the house.

I still cannot recall who the other person was, or if there were more than two, but I vividly remember that the man on the driver's seat was my father! I came to learn even that fact only after he had come back to see me a few more times; on these subsequent occasions, my mother would say, 'Get ready; go and greet your father.' It dawned on me then that the man who came to the house very occasionally (he had another wife) with sweets, bread, and dresses for all the three of us was actually not my father. What I remember of him is that he loved me as he did my sisters and treated us the same during the times (sometimes a few days) when he visited.

The confusion about why my father only occasionally came to greet me from the car and went away after a short time was later eased a bit when my mother gradually told me a few things. So with time, I figured out she had met my step father when I was a baby, and he'd who accepted

3

her with her baby, but he also had another wife. Polygamy was, back then more than now, acceptable in our society, and probably this arrangement was convenient more for her than for him, as not many men would have wanted to marry a girl who had had another man's child. Today I believe, my mother could easily have had a husband of her own because she was, and still is, a pretty woman, despite her age and a few problems and minor ailments.

Later, more children were born, but unfortunately by the time their good dad passed away, he and my mother were not really 'good friends' anymore. He had sold off the house he had built for her, and in which I had once lived, and my mother had gone to live with her mother, just across the road.

I do not exactly remember for how long I lived with my grandma, but when I was about six years old, she told me that there were arrangements for me to be taken to live with my father. I guess it was probably because I was nervous about moving to a world of the unknown, but the first time she broke the news to me I cried throughout the night. An older cousin with whom I shared a bed comforted me and told me that my father was a rich man and that I was going to be happier. I have no regrets, though quite frankly I know riches and happiness do not necessarily go together. I was happy, all right, but for completely different reasons.

To me, the general belief that a stepmother is the worst person on the planet is completely false. Believe me, stepchildren have a very big part to play in how their step-parents relate to them. Fathers, too, could have their share of the blame in the whole game. The excessive love my father has for me even now could have been a recipe for confusion in our home, but on the whole, all of us have played our cards right.

One afternoon, I had to leave my grandmother, mother, sisters, and brothers, and it seemed to be ceremonious because my maternal uncles—I don't remember how many—were there to escort me, a few other relatives came to see me off, and my father had brought people with him as well. Also, there was more than one car. From that time on, my rightful home was my father's; I went to see my mother occasionally, but only as a visitor. She gets annoyed that I don't remember most of her relatives, but indeed I don't know them and it is not my fault. I loved my grandmother so much and was there to bury her when she passed away twenty years later. Sometimes I wish she were still living, so I could spoil her the way she did me. She offered me whatever it was in her powers to offer—it was not much, but I look back with a lot of appreciation. It made a difference. All children deserve to be loved, or they will grow up not knowing how to love other people.

CHAPTER 2

Children are innocent, and they should be protected from intrigue, hatred, jealously and other evils if we are all to make a difference in this world. How I wish people could strive to make this world a better place to live in!

By the time the uncles who had accompanied me were leaving to go back, I was out in the compound playing with the boys—the brothers I had never met before that day. I had learnt that they were Patrick and Richard only that afternoon, but I took off to play hide and seek and football as if I had known them all my life. That was the beginning of another life. We have since been inseparable!

I will never stop laughing when I remember my father stopping me from making the sign of the cross on my forehead, chest, and shoulders before and after eating. Naturally, that's what I did when dinner was served the evening I arrived. I had been baptized and brought up by my strong Catholic mother, and here I was in my father's equally strong Anglican home. Later, I was taken to church and formally initiated into the Anglican faith. This was at the time of my confirmation and Holy Communion. I never made the sign of the cross again except for fun. Now that I am grown up, I make the sign whenever I attend ceremonies in the Catholic Church or pray with my mum.

Fortunately, I did not have to change my name. Thank God my mother had not called me Immaculate or Consolata!! I actually share a name with my paternal auntie, so Beatrice is neither Catholic nor Anglican. It may not even be Christian at all, I don't really know.

My grandmother had been right; this environment was very different in so many aspects. There were too many dos and don'ts, strict rules on timekeeping for each of the dos and punishment for the don'ts. We bathed on time, ate on time, and went to bed on time, almost like robots. Dad dropped us off at school on time before he drove to work and came back on time. I live this way even now. I know that if each activity is done in its proper time, it will not eat into the time of the next. By following this rule, a person can live a life that is more organized and smooth-running.

We had workers for both the housework and the outside chores, but for anything that concerned the children, Mum—Akiiki—took personal charge. From the time she got married, she never went back to being employed; she had been a secondary school teacher. She was a full-time housewife, and my God, how she enjoyed what she was doing. While my father went to work, she was in-charge of the house, the workers, the tea shambas, the dairy farm, and all of us. Sometimes I think all this contributed to the high blood pressure she developed, because she was (and still is) a perfectionist.

At the time, a family lived on whatever the breadwinner earned. It was so much different from now, when the cost of living is so high that both spouses have to hit the road for work, and everyone wants to make as much as possible in the shortest time. Many people do not earn enough, or so they think, and some live beyond their means. This explains the corruption in government offices, the theft in private businesses, the lack of trust (on financial matters) among couples, and the grabbing, grabbing, and grabbing by children, relatives, employees—name it. The belief now is that the end justifies the means, and what is the end? Wealth. The means—anything—includes child sacrifice, immoral sexual behaviour, robbery, and ... the list is long.

CHAPTER 3

We went to Kiburara Primary School, which was about one mile from home. My grandfather's farm was separated from the school by a fence, and my uncle's farm was next to my grandfather's. The land on which the school was built had been donated to the community by my grandfather, as was the church, which is next door to the school, on the other side. The old man had acquired a lot of land, which he later gave out to his many children. He not only knew the value of land and how it would appreciate with time, but also knew the value education.

I joined the school in primary class two, joining my brother Patrick. I do not know why I was made to repeat this class, because I had already finished primary class two in the school where my mum taught. Certainly I could not have been substandard, because no interview was conducted. Someone just decided that I had to repeat the class. I suspect it was my father. While today we know exactly at what age a student should be in which class, in those days there was no such standardization. In one class, you could easily find students with ages ranging from seven to fifteen. After all, some people say, age is just a number. They could be right, because some much older children in our class were not necessarily brighter. My other brother Richard was in the class behind ours, and we had a baby sister Lilly still at home.

Even back then, I knew that to be an achiever you had to compete. To compete favourably you needed to be on top of situations. At that time, students were not just pushed from one class to another to create room for others. If one did not do well, one would be made to repeat a class. We studied and learnt both at school and at home, so my brother and I were above average in performance. A family's set-up and the home environment definitely affect and influence performance in school. I know that children who have to fetch water and firewood for dinner may not do as well as those who find tea ready, bathe, rest, and commit the rest of the evening to revising their school notes. Candlelight or a lantern is not as good as electric light, and sometimes people run out of gas, interrupting children's reading. We actually had no excuse for not performing well because we were comparatively privileged, for which I thank God.

This did not auger well with some of the children and even some of the teachers in our school. It took me a long time to understand that class differentials caused hatred among people. In fact, this resentment was so deep-rooted that a misfortune in our family would be a source of celebration to others around us. While we very much wanted to be friendly and play with other children, they always had harsh and unkind words for us. I later learnt and accepted that superiority and inferiority are not mere myths; they are real and each may hurt, but in a different way. I now take comfort in the fact that each can be well managed to minimize the extent of vulnerability. One is at fault if one fails to learn to manage the effects of either of those complexes.

CHAPTER 4

In 1975, my brother and I joined Nyakasura School, a boarding school at the foot of the Rwenzori Mountains in Fort Portal. It was prestigiously referred to as 'the school'. My father had studied at the same school but at a time when just boys studied there.

The reactions of young children being separated from their parents vary from child to child. Surprisingly, my reaction was to be immensely excited! For some reason, I was happy to be 'independent'. It was such an experience meeting other children from different parts of Uganda, listening to other languages, and hearing about practices in different cultures. This was a diversity I had not experienced before, or even imagined.

Moral education in schools like this one, founded by missionaries, was a priority. Attending Chapel every morning was an integral part of the school curriculum. It is not surprising that by the end of the first term of the first year, most students are 'saved' or 'born again'. Some backslide later, others continue, and a few remain indifferent. I was no exception to the wave. By the middle of the term, I was already saved, had joined the choir and the Young Women Christians Association (YWCA), and periodically took readings in the Chapel. I joined a 'club', where senior students who'd been saved and some teachers acted as our spiritual leaders. They organized prayer meetings, fellowships, and conventions. We were introduced to fasting, which never caught up with me as far as I can remember.

Towards the end of my second year in secondary school, I abandoned the 'saved' group because of what I saw as a double standard and manipulation by our seniors. One guy who was extremely saved—at least by our standards—told me that God had, through angels and dreams, sent him a message that He (God) had chosen me for this senior colleague.

He had had that vision for seven days in a row, he said, and now wanted to pray and fast about with me about it. For the rest, God would take control. As we prayed, he tried to kiss me. I was shocked! I later actually learnt that there were a number of other 'saved' colleagues who had paired up, and the rumour among the students was that most did not practice what they preached. There were some who were genuine and serious who remained saved through school, university, and after. This senior colleague and brother in Christ pestered me so much that at one point I felt that I was being disobedient to God Himself. The more I went back for prayer meetings, the more I hated what I saw; slowly I lost interest until I stopped. Quietly I pulled out of the group and continued in the choir for two more years. I grappled with the idea of giving a testimony and exposing these things, but after some time, I decided not to do it.

For the following two years of my O level, I spent much of my time in boys' company. Having grown up with boys, I found girls' company monotonous, with discussions limited to narrow subjects like hair, dresses, and boyfriends—some imaginary. I learnt that some of the girls had already had affairs with fellow students as well as teachers. In fact, some dropped out of school because of early pregnancies. The bigger girls in A level were more sophisticated and it was like we were miles apart. I kept with my friends—the boys—as I still do, and learnt so much from them about what they think of girls and also how vulnerable the boys themselves are. I learnt to act like boys—being rough and tough. They protected me as if I were their treasured, sister and for this I am forever grateful, because I it helped form part of my character and my outlook towards life. I am not rough and tough now, but I am probably more open-minded.

CHAPTER 5

The political situation Uganda when I was in school was bad, with stories of President Amin and his henchmen killing and abducting outstanding people. There was general acrimony; even as students, we started hating the regime. At the beginning of every term, our colleagues—particularly those who came from Kampala—had so many stories to tell about the atrocities. Some had parents and family members who had disappeared without a trace. Many had lost parents and relatives at the hands of the dictator. Those students whose parents were 'in the system' stood out because of the way they dressed, talked, and danced, and the amount of money and food they brought! They were the talk of the school. Today, I cannot quite figure out where they went, because I don't see many of them in town.

The seriousness of the political situation dawned on us when some senior public servants started getting murdered or 'disappeared', even in our small Fort Portal town. Two of the prominent men who were killed worked with my father when he was the Public Works Supervisor for the Western Region. This was frightening to us as a family as it was getting closer, and almost certainly he would be the next. Most of the political talk was done in whispers and away from the children, but when it became evident that my father was a likely target, we could see and feel the tension at home. Every day when my father went to work, we were not certain he would come back. Any stranger seen near our home was a source of worry and concern. It was a trying time, and I believe many families went to exile. My father braved it out, and thank God he survived, by sheer luck.

The economy deteriorated so much, most essentials—soap, kerosene, sugar, salt—became rare commodities because factories had closed, especially after Amin chased away Asians who owned and ran most industries. Favourites of the Government were allocated big Asian businesses to manage, but could not cope because they lacked the business skills and acumen. There was rationing of everything in shops, and it followed at home. I remember during one period in our home, sugar was mixed in our tea centrally. The scarcity of petrol and diesel almost caused a problem for my father, because soldiers would always demand that he give them fuel that was meant for public civil works. With hindsight, I think Amin's soldiers believed they had the right to anything—public or private. Just like their commander-in-chief, they could even humiliate men by taking away their wives from them in broad daylight. The men were lucky if they were killed after their wives were taken. It was clear that the bad situation was getting worse by the day, and it was unimaginable that anyone would be able to stop it. In fact, when the assault on Amin started, the regime became even more brutal, and most Ugandans prayed for the war against Amin to stop, lest the whole population become extinct as pressure mounted on him and his regime. The fall of Idi Amin is still vivid in my mind, and I remember very sadly that at Kyebambe Girls School, where I'd gone in 1979 for my A Levels, some of the girls who did not manage to run out of school and go home were raped by Amin's soldiers. The rest—how the liberators took over, one President after another, the elections of 1980—is history known to most people. One thing I will not forget, however, is that I led a political student movement to join the new Uganda Patriotic Movement (UPM) led by now-President Museveni. I still hold onto my Party Card No. 34461 very dearly. ON 19 July 1980, the party leadership held a public rally at Nyakaseke in Fort Portal, where most students from schools around enrolled in the party and received party cards. It was an exciting period of campaigns, lasting until December, when elections were held. I am not very sure I know what became of my first cherished party—UPM, but now I hold the card of another party— NRM (National Resistance Movement)—whose programme is similar to the Sixteen Aims and Objectives of UPM, which I had crammed by heart. NRM is the child or grandchild of UPM.

CHAPTER 6

Nyakasura school's glory did not survive the negative changes that took place in the country at that time. While other schools and colleges seem to have recovered, I am afraid Nyakasura did not quite. In fact, the school that was once one of the best in the country is little heard of now. In academic performance, sports and games, or drama and singing—name it, a lot needs to be done. As old students, we have formed an association that is determined to restore the lost glory of the school.

Besides academics, Nyakasura emphasized discipline, morals, and general etiquette. The headmaster then, Mr. Moses Nyakazingo, even taught boys how to ask a girl for a dance and escort her back to her seat after. We were taught how to handle eating utensils, and boys were shown how to tie their ties. The emphasis was on keeping simple, but modest and clean. Most of all, we were taught to be respectful to other people. We learned fast because we were also taught to listen. At the end of the day, we can learn something good from all human beings—if we listen with open minds.

At Nyakasura School, we were taught to respect authority as well as to develop our own leadership skills. This is a virtue that made a contribution to the lives of many who went through the school, especially when I went and before. The school motto speaks for itself: It is honourable to serve and not to be served, to minister and not be ministered unto. To me, this can be extended to the pleasure I get by giving rather than receiving. Whatever little I have, I have had the pleasure to share it with the less fortunate. This has not always been material things, but information, knowledge, and ideas.

I look back with respect and adoration to the only three girls who were in Form Six when I was in Form One—Peace Ruhindi, Rosette Kyampaire and Naome (now Mrs. Kato)—smart, responsible, and respectable. The same great Senior Six class also had David Tinyefuza, David Rusa, and Modest Kanyunyizi—great debators who later became lawyers—and Richard Buteera, now Director of Public Prosecution, a class below. In Form Four were people who mentored us and for whom I still have a lot of respect—Hannington Karuhanga, Benon Biraaro, John Kazoora, and Bariyo Barigye, who later died during Uganda's liberation struggle in the bush. Although I moved to another school for A Level, I kept in close contact with friends and former classmates at Nyakasura. At the end of our two years in A Level, only five girls from my O Level class made it to Makerere University. I am happy that we remained friends with all of them, Grace Kazooba (Mrs Nyakahuma), Dorothy Mwirumubi (Mrs Baguma), Juliet Karegyesa (Mrs. Byabage), and Monica Makoro (may she rest in peace). A few of the other girls who did not make it to University along with us have been successful in different ways. The AIDS scourge and other causes have robbed us of some former classmates, both girls and boys, but on the whole, I meet many male former classmates in professional fields, both within the country and outside. Besides where we are working and what we are doing when we meet, we now talk about children, and for some, grandchildren. How nice it is!

CHAPTER 7

Makerere University was fun in 1981. Away from the parental restrictions at home and harsh rules and regulations at school, a whole new world opened up right in front of me. There was a variety of characters to deal with, both in the residence halls and the lecture rooms. The students who had been in single sex schools found more difficulty integrating in a society where boys and girls visited each other in the residence halls. Some even walked hand-in-hand, with the more courageous (and probably spoilt) even kissing and having sex. There was no dress code, no roll call, no restrictions on drinking and smoking, and no curfew. It was a new experience that taught us something, and it called for the values we had earlier learnt of self-control and restraint to be applied. There were no sanctions for what would previously have drawn punitive action. Students from urban elite families mixed with rural, timid, and inexperienced ones. The scope was as varied as nature itself. There was going to be a lot of decision-making to do here and a lot of choices to make.

My friends and I decided to keep to the rules we'd been used to, breaking them sometimes here and there without going to extremes and suffering the repercussions we very well knew. There were some senior girls we became friends with, but wherever appropriate we would retract and reflect on some of their actions. Sharing a room with Juliet made a big difference to me because we knew each other, had a lot in common, and as much as possible, made plans together—mostly visiting one uncle or aunt over the weekends, strategizing on how to spend our pocket money, choosing which party to attend, and most important, discussing how to remain decent in the free and non-restrictive atmosphere.

We differed from a few of our colleagues in that the enormous freedom also increased our realization of vulnerability and sense of responsibility over ourselves. The level to which some girls had stooped to acquire material things from older men was, to say the least, disgusting, but it was comforting to know that this was another breed and we did not have to copy and paste their behaviour. If it was not my Uncle Ben or Auntie Dinah inviting us for lunch, it was Juliet's Uncle Sam, Uncle Andrew, or cousin Frank (all now deceased) taking us out for a drink or a meal. We had the basics. Uncle Robert would spoil me with lots of money whenever he was in town (from Northern Uganda, where he was based in the army). Now I know that sometimes people do things not because they enjoy them or because they want to, but because of what they are lacking and what they will get in return. It is dangerous and unfortunate, but also true. Unfortunately, the trend has spread and caught up with most young girls, especially in the higher institutions of learning today.

Even without being policed, one thing I knew was that I had to pass with a good degree. I enjoyed my classes, especially economics—I still enjoy it; I also enjoyed the parties on campus, especially the Freshers' and Leavers' Balls. We made more friends, and the students with whom I was at University in different years and courses are today the ones holding high offices in both public and private sectors, though a wave of younger professionals is catching up with us very fast. All in all, meeting contemporaries is always a refreshing experience. Sometimes, even when I cannot put a name to a face, as soon as I find that 'we were together at campus', talk turns to the residence halls, our courses, changes at Makerere University, and I feel very comfortable. The talk about who married whom, how many children we have, and what we have done since University brings the frightening realization that we are growing old and should probably start thinking about retirement.

PART II

11th October, 2006: Tomorrow is my birthday, and here I am alone, away from family and friends, in a hotel room in Dar es Salaam, staring at the television but not really following the news on CNN. It's something about global warming and gas emissions. Not that I would have celebrated my birthday in any particular style, but at least the children would have sung for me, or proposed a dinner or something more interesting. My mind races through so many things—probably an account of my forty-five years—and then I remember I had at one time begun writing a book. I cannot quite remember how far I had gotten, but I decided that I needed to separate this book into certain episodes of my life.

Many things are happening in my life right now. As usual, I am determined to see how I can use them to make a difference to other people as well as to myself.

A person has just called me who has been calling religiously many times a day. He says he loves me very much and seems to be slowly opening that part of me which has been dormant for a long time; a very exciting experience. The other excitement in my life right now is the reason I am in Dar es Salaam, to attend the launching of the National Consultative process to seek people's views on the proposed Political Federation of East Africa—Kenya, Uganda, and Tanzania. This is the task to which I was specifically appointed by the three heads of state six months ago. I am working hard to have the political federation succeed. If it does, that will be a whole chapter in my life's experiences and a difference in the lives of about 100 million people in East Africa.

CHAPTER 8

The class of 1981 at Makerere University, for those like me who were doing three-year courses, finished in 1984, but graduation was scheduled for January 1985. Graduation, as usual, was a period of excitement, with a lot of celebration around Kampala and beyond. The end of student life was exciting, but for most people it was also the beginning of another life—that of uncertainty. It usually dawns on you at some point after the ceremonies that there is no more free food and accommodation. In the case of Uganda, then as now, it is the beginning of long painful period of job-seeking, having to put up with sometimes no-so-welcoming relatives, high expectations quickly being deflated, and for girls sometimes getting involved in relationships they do not really want. You come face-to-face with the reality that out there, no one really cares whether you have a degree, or even what grades you scored. You have to fend for yourself if you are to remain relevant.

At the time of my graduation, there was a class of people who dealt in all sorts of businesses—most speculative and some illegal—and had so much money, at least by our standards, that they took pleasure in spiting those that had studied but had no jobs and no income. Because of this, some young men chose to start trading businesses rather than waste time going for useless and worthless degrees. Some young women chose to become second, third, or fourth wives of wealthy businessmen who could not speak a sentence of English, but put food on the table. It was a battle for survival, and battles usually leave most people dirty.

Almost all industries were owned by the government by then, after they'd been nationalized following Idi Amin, and therefore they were mismanaged and producing below capacity. At graduation parties, one needed a chit allocating beer or soda, or even the Uganda Gin, Waragi. The allocations were not enough, forcing us to buy some drinks at very high prices on the *black market*. Allocations were a privilege of those who had 'connections' with people in government. Most graduates depended for their parties on drinks bought from the second or third buyer at almost twice the factory price, but parties had to be made, or so everyone thought. Talk about social pressure.

My graduation party was a good one, because my uncle Robert was in the army and could get some drinks from the army shop, and another uncle, Ben could get the spirits cheaply from importers since his wife was one. I also managed to get one allocation and to pay for another that the allocatee could not pay for. It was a joint party for me and my cousin Edward at the residence of my late Uncle Victor, who was then a Permanent Secretary. It was the usual—eating, drinking, dancing, speeches—but at the end of it all, I had no job. I was, granted, better off than some colleagues who were putting up with distant relatives, because I was fully catered for by my uncle and very close friend Robert, to whom I am eternally grateful for his having mentored me. I was also protected from the claws of old men in government and outside, looking for young girls to befriend by promising to get them jobs. I had free food and accommodation, beers when I wanted, and the freedom to invite friends to partake of the same at my uncle's house.

All in all, unemployment affected many of the graduates, some of whom took to doing odd jobs to survive. But as the saying goes, when the going is good, the good look even better; when it gets tough, the bad get rough—opening a whole can of worms. A lot of illegal things were being done, morality did not have much meaning, and most people had crossed the line where morals and integrity were concerned. It became common practice for government officials to ask for bribes or 'sell' Government information, even when it was an entitlement to the public. When there was nothing to sell, people supplied 'air' and the government bought it. Corruption was rampant at all levels of Ugandan society. Civil servants would leave jackets on the backs of their office chairs, giving the impression they were in the office, and go down town to try to trade in something to make ends meet. Because of a lack of paper bags, Government office messengers stole files and sold those papers; sometimes 'confidential' files were used to wrap bread or nuts or popcorn.

People could easily kill for so little. Life did not really matter as long as some people remained on top. In all of this, there were clear participants and victims, creating in some a false sense of superiority. This falsehood also manifested itself in a sense of deep-rooted fear and insecurity, which was expressed in different ways; some leaders feared even their own shadows. There was a lot of suspicion, back-stabbing, and lies to create favouritism among the political leadership. I can now comfortably say that the higher you climb, the harder you hit the ground when you fall. This also explains why I cannot see most of those students I was with in Nyasura school who ate, dressed, and lived differently from most of us.

Slowly the brain-drain, which had started during Idi Amin's reign, continued. Intellectuals and professionals were careful not to make those above them in government uncomfortable by displaying a lot of talent, lest they stir up insecurity, resentment, and envy. I have since come to believe that it is not a weakness to disguise your strengths by letting others outshine you. You remain in control, because it is the natural course of things that power eventually fades and weakens. Intellectuals took to drinking, confidence was undermined, and high levels of frustration caused unexplained deaths—it was chaotic. Today, it all sounds like a bad dream to those who experienced it and fiction to those who did not. Describing this era in the history of my beloved country makes me sad, especially when I describe it to the younger people who are today taking so much for granted. We should not abuse the process that brought us this far.

CHAPTER 9

Eventually I got a job in a private consultancy firm, Serefaco, after a year of serious job-seeking. I got little pay, but I was content with the fact that I woke up to go to work every morning. My situation was not comparable to those of other friends, because I was entirely provided for. Working was a good experience, and I took my job seriously. My belief has always been that when you take on a responsibility, you give it your all or else don't take it at all.

At the close of that year, the political situation grew tenser, with an imminent military coup over the Obote regime. The chief of staff Oyite Ojok died in a plane crash, and this was the beginning of more trouble. I do not want to serialize the events involving the new chief of staff, Smith Opon Acan, the other players like Bazilio Olal Okello, the military coup on the Obote regime by Tito Okello Lutwa, and other incidents that preceded the takeover, finally, by NRA. There were too many factions as well as alliances, with some more powerful than others. There were invisible walls between and among senior military personnel and government officials; most remained hanging in there because the future that they looked forward to seemed very empty. The fall was coming, and very fast. Alliances started changing; the song was not in tandem with the beat. There was total chaos. The fragile partnerships started to have visible cracks, people started claiming they had good intentions, but good intentions were not good enough. They needed to be followed by accountability—and not many people in leadership were ready for that. The clock could not be rewound; it was ticking and time was up. The political landscape was about to change, and no one was sure whether change would be for the better. The best we all could hope for was that it would happen sooner rather than later.

Some people failed to give up dreaming, up to the last minute before the government was finally run over. They insisted they were not losing, but could not say they were winning. The sad fact, but a fact nonetheless, was that events were increasingly moving beyond their control, and nothing would stop this significant new reality.

CHAPTER 10

As the liberation movement intensified, advancing towards capturing power in 1985, Kampala city became a mixture of so many things. The military turned its anger and desperation on the population, torturing, raping, and killing innocent civilians. Almost every day there was a scare in town, leading people to run in different directions while thieves and robbers took advantage. The economy was almost at a standstill; the civil service experienced a temporary halt. The west of Uganda had fallen to the (rebel) liberators, while the rest of the country remained in the hands of the government. This situation added to the tension, because most civilians and even soldiers whose origins were in the western region were suspected to be collaborators of the 'enemy'. At this point, the uncle with whom I lived defected and joined the 'rebel' army ranks in western Uganda. This put my own life in danger, because his colleagues in the Uganda National Liberation Army (UNLA) thought I knew something and could provide some answers. For some days, I was to go underground , but the instructions I had were to leave the army house without arousing suspicion, with only my basic necessities so as not to attract attention. I was to tell no one, not even my uncle's friend and colleague who lived with us. I went through one of the hardest times of my life from the hour my uncle left at about five in the morning to nine o'clock, when his colleague left for work. I had not slept all night, but I was fully awake and alert. I had to avoid making a wrong move so as not to get myself into trouble, but I did not know how to do this, given that I could not estimate how much time I had to play with before anyone at the army headquarters a few blocks away suspected. The idea of leaving the house with my suitcase, with everything intact as if I would be coming back in the evening looked simple, but the more I thought about it, the more unattractive it looked.

I thought about our housemate, Lieutenant Ouma, being killed because of suspected connivance with Robert. How could he explain the defection of a colleague with whom he shared a house? Today I wonder whether this was a naive morality question, putting my own survival below another person's, but though I was strictly told not to mention a thing to him, this was an instruction I started revisiting as soon as my uncle left. I never gave him the full details of what transpired. The situation I was in did not require good intentions, integrity, or a fairly acceptable moral ground; it was one of those moments when people see but choose to be blind, hear but choose to be deaf. Whatever the case, I had to do something, and very fast. The options were not many.

I made two decisions whose price could have been too high and could have been shared by many other people. Once I confirmed (through means I'll not mention here) that my uncle was out of government territory, I decided to make my first move. I would spend the night packing his personal belongings and mine, but the following day, I would tell Lieutenant Ouma the truth about the defection. Before I told Ouma I would have emptied our bedrooms (which were upstairs), leaving the sitting and dining rooms downstairs intact. After I disclosed the plan to Ouma, if he himself did not kill me, I'd get a truck the following morning as soon as he went to work, pack the rest of everything, and leave. This was all well worked out in my mind, and I rehearsed the plan over and over; it looked neat and smart. If it did not go smoothly the repercussions were clear. I made a conscious effort to shut possible failure out of my mind and failed miserably. I kept pacing back and forth in the house, but I was also strengthening my resolve.

CHAPTER 11

Honesty is a blunt instrument; it does not make you win people's hearts. In fact, it is sometimes offensive. People easily mistake sincerity with honesty, but the former can be demonstrated with successfully deceptive facial expressions, while the latter cannot. That evening I chose to be sincere rather than honest. I did not tell Lieutenant Ouma that our bedrooms upstairs were cleared and that I had been part of the defection plot. Rather I told him, with genuine tears, that Robert, who had supposedly gone to see his ailing father, had arrived safely but had been captured by the rebel forces. It was unlikely they would kill him, but almost certain he would not make it back. The ensuing conversation was so tough and emotional, but I knew I had to go through it in the little time left. I knew for sure the following morning Ouma would report this information and they would come for me to testify, to explain how I knew about the capture of my uncle, since the west of Uganda was cut off and there was no communication. I was not ready for that, so I had to act, and fast. I did not need more thinking and planning. I had done a lot of that, and I had no more decisions to make, either because I had already made them or because my options were sealed.

My relatives did not want to risk their lives if I was found at one of their houses, so the few I approached indicated politely that they would not have me at their homes. One cousin offered to keep the first batch of stuff I got out of the house but warned that I should not be seen taking more to her place. Fair enough, I would have been lighter if I had taken my uncle's instructions to leave everything in the house. I had chosen otherwise, so I had to get somewhere else to keep the rest—stuff from the kitchen, sitting room, and dining room that I stupidly was determined to carry away early the following morning as soon as Ouma left. I managed to get someone's garage to store these things, and by 9:00 a.m. was disconnecting the fridge and cooker, so that by the time the soldiers came about 11:00 a.m., I had left with the truck and was a safe distance away.

When I reached my destination, I called the house land line (there were no mobiles) and our house boy told me that I was a wanted person and that even Lieutenant Ouma was now spitting fire, cursing his friend Robert (who had given him free accommodation for almost one year) and swearing he would shoot him if he ever saw him again. Unfortunately, the two never met again, because Ouma's health was not so good and he passed away within the first year after the liberation, before the two had a chance to meet again.

My own misadventure had placed me in a crisis of my own making. I should not have told Ouma so early, before I knew where I was going to safely stay myself. With hindsight, I did not have to be so materialistic, choosing to carry all of my uncle's belongings out of the house. I could not stay with the two people who had agreed to keep the things for me. I could not allow myself to be traced, together with the household items, because then those people would also be in danger. I had to find different accommodation altogether, and at that moment I did not know where, exactly. I felt I had the obligation to tell whoever would accommodate me the truth. The reality is, I was like a robber on the run.

My uncle and I had had many friends, and I took the whole day doing a checklist and looking for the least obvious, where I could not be found quickly if I was followed. I approached one lady friend who was working in the Central Bank, owned a flat by herself, and did not come from the same part of the country as I did. I had earlier borrowed a spare tyre from her for the inconspicuous vehicle my uncle used. Peace Magabo was very sympathetic, understanding, so comforting, ready and willing to put me up unconditionally. I will forever be indebted to her. Though at some point we ceased being very close, I always pray that one day, while we both live, I will have an opportunity to do something for her that no one else would.

I moved in with Peace at the Bank of Uganda flats (now Speke Apartments, Wampewo Avenue). I stayed in her apartment when she went abroad to England for medical reasons for almost a year. We had a relationship which for many reasons was fragile, and as soon as I realized this, I had to play my cards right. I had to find a balance between the possible extremes and toe the line that worked best for me, avoiding outright arguments or disagreements. It worked, so I do not remember any dramatic failures in our relationship. I kept reminding myself, however, that Peace was my friend but really owed me nothing and had no responsibility over me, or an obligation to keep me happy. She was also entitled to her moods. I think I invaded her space for enough time, if not too long.

PART III

Past errors cannot be undone. They will be there, live with us and we with them, but if we are humble enough to accept responsibility for our own actions, attempt to regain control and find a way to proceed, then the possibility is strong that sometimes we will hurt, but only temporarily. The longer we wait to take decisions, the more difficult it becomes. Uncertainty and the fear of the unknown can cause frustration, keeping a lid on tensions that will continue to grow. It is not difficult to imagine that a situation has changed from what it was or what it ought to be. To face it as it is and give up dreaming is a bold step that takes a determination that most people lack.

CHAPTER 12

I had introduced a boyfriend to my uncle before all those things happened. It was not long before I also told him I did not want anything to do with that boyfriend anymore because he was somewhat irresponsible; he drank and lacked seriousness. That affair had ended, and there were no hard feelings or serious regrets. Each of us later moved on, and we are still friendly when we meet.

The emptiness I experienced and felt during the time immediately after my uncle left also brought with it a deep sense of insecurity. I did not know how long I would have to be put up by my friend. My parents were now cut off in the west of Uganda under a different government regime; communication was almost not there. The most significant new reality by any reasonable definition was that I had lost the protection of my parents, my uncle, and my family that I had enjoyed all my life. I had not had such enormous freedom in my life before, but I also had the vulnerability of manoeuvring through things alone. I had always been protected; now I felt exposed. Though in a way I was enjoying the freedom and independence, I was scared at the same time. It had come too abruptly and I did not really know how to be out there all by myself. I kept mindful of the dos and the don'ts that I had been taught since childhood. It was a strange situation. I was an adult girl, a graduate, working and scared of too much freedom, a different kind of freedom from the one I experienced at University.

My brother Patrick was still at University, but unlike me, in holidays he lived with our Aunt Dinah, who was a very good guardian. Richard had finished University and was at home with our parents when our part of the country fell to the freedom fighters. Patrick and I kept close, seeing each other as much as possible. I could also now afford to give him a little pocket money or take him out for a drink once in a while. Still it was not the same as when they had come to my uncle's for weekends. There had been a sudden change in my life, but I had no choice except to hang in there.

CHAPTER 13

In 1985, I met the man I later married. I do not remember the month. Within a short time we had become very close. We were in love and happy to be with each other as much as possible. One big hassle I remember he relieved me of was boarding the public-transport minibuses to and from work. He would pass by the flat where I stayed in Wampewo and give me a ride to work and pick me up after work and take me home or take me out before taking me home. In a way, Steven bridged a gap in my life, and my friend Peace saw less and less of me. He was five years older than I, had been working longer, and had just returned from a post-graduate course in the United Kingdom, resuming work at his job with the Uganda Electricity Board. Steven is an electrical engineer. I know he loved me dearly, and I loved him. He had a gentle way of expressing his feelings, and the little nice things he did made me feel good. By all standards, Steven was a handsome man, and well built, but he did not have much of a sense of humour. I suspected it had to do with his profession, and that did not bother me, really, as he enjoyed my sense of humour. We introduced to each other our friends and some family members, and as we went along I was convinced there were no secrets between us. Fortunately for me, I had very few skeletons in my closet if any even qualified to be called that. As far as I can remember, I put everything on the table, something I consider to be very important in relationships. It is not a sacrifice; instead it makes me feel better, lighter if you wish, because I do not have the energy to carry the heavy burden of secrets—some unnecessary. I would be too scared of being found out and being considered dishonest, selfish, and insincere. In the same vein, those are qualities I would least want to entertain in a partner. The discomfort of having to exchange information on major as well as minor issues can be draining and diversionary, and may in most cases cause resentment or a deep feeling of betrayal. I assumed, or wanted to believe that my boyfriend had also put all that mattered in our relationship on the table. He never asked me about ex-boyfriends and I did not offer information, but he voluntarily told me about two past affairs of his and they sounded like the usual pastimes and did not bother me at all. I knew one of the girls casually and I wondered how he could have had an affair with her, but he had said it was so short and nothing really serious.

CHAPTER 14

For about ten days before Kampala finally fell to the National Resistance Army, there was a lot of shelling and gun fire, dead bodies littered the city, and contingents of soldiers could visibly be seen fleeing the city towards the East of Uganda. We had to store a lot of dry food, because shops and markets would not open and no one knew how long this would take. People stayed indoors. Some brave hooligans took to the streets, breaking into shops to loot. The fleeing soldiers also stole, killed people, raped women, and destroyed buildings.

We all waited for this to end so we could be reunited with our families; I could not wait to see my Uncle Robert again. At one time, he had been rumoured killed in one of the towns in Western Uganda, but later I learnt that he was alive and well. I could not wait to introduce Steven to my parents, and he could not wait to take me as his wedded wife, to love, to cherish, and to hold. He had proposed and I had accepted; to me, that was all that mattered. I was twenty-five and ready to start my own family.

My friendship with Peace was fading as fast as the one with Steven was growing. The two relationships were, in a way, inversely proportional to each other. Clearly, I had to make a choice. Fortunately, I now had Steven to share all this frustration with. He came up with a quick solution, and it could not have come at a better time. I was really at the edge of my patience. I was exhausted with trying to be good, and I could not understand why this was happening. Whatever the reason, it happened, and whenever I kept quiet or went away, thinking it was the best defence, it ended up being a great offence. Nothing I did pleased my friend anymore.

When I was ready to move, I thanked Peace for having put me up and for all the nice things she had done for me. I packed my things and left for the Imperial Hotel, where Steven had booked me a room to stay until I found a house to rent. Within two weeks, I had found the house and moved to a house on Clement Hill Road. I was actually moving in to a two bedroom guest wing, just enough for me. It would do until I got married (soon) and moved in with my husband. He visited often, so I was not lonely.

Meanwhile, the NRA had taken over, and my uncle was back in town. It was a very happy moment for us, a memorable reunion. We had a lot to catch up on, and he was amazed when I informed him that as soon as he got a house I would bring all his household items. He was shocked by some of my stories, amused by others, and evidently take aback by this boyfriend thing. He made no effort to hide it. What I realized, and he did not, was that he was trying to regain the control he had lost. I liked my uncle and respected him. He had strong opinions, but most times we shared them or discussed them until we reach a compromise. Clearly, on this one, what was obvious was that I did not need an opinion and was ready to take responsibility for my decision and actions. He tactfully took the only available option, to rest his case. His reservation arose from the fact that this was someone he did not know and had met before. We did not even know Steven's family. I could not answer him back out of respect, but inside I asked myself if my uncle thought he knew all Ugandans. Anyway he got on board and I was happy, because I cherished his friendship and his contribution to my life, not only as an uncle but as a friend. The thought of a disagreement with him was scary, but I had become very bold. Within a year, he was introducing us to his fiancée. I was very happy for him for having found such a wonderful person for a wife, because he, too, is a wonderful person. They are a great match, both different from one another and the same; a mix I cannot explain. Doreen is a combination of many qualities. She is a blessing to my dear uncle and to the entire family; she is also a great friend of mine.

CHAPTER 15

As soon as it was safe to travel, I took a trip home to see my parents. They were in good health and had good stories about the liberators: how well behaved the soldiers from the 'bush' were and how funny and interesting Museveni (the leader of the revolution and now president) was. The people in that part of the country were one regime behind us in Kampala, because by the time Tito Okello Lutwa overthrew Obote's regime, they were already under NRA rule.

I also had a lot to share with my family. I was particularly eager to see my grandfather, whom we all loved so much. He was full of wisdom and very analytical, but also very critical. He had some ailments but was still strong and very alert. Well above ninety, he spent most of his time reading the Bible, occasionally taking a walk on his farm. His letters to me reminded me of pen pals we had in school, except his were both poetic and meaningful, with a great sense of humour and a lot of wise counsel. Up to the time he passed away, my grandfather enclosed some money in each letter he wrote to me; in the last, he sent me money to buy milk for my baby. In an uncharacteristic act for a parent or grandparent, he had also encouraged me in the same letter to leave my husband and go back home, where I had always been and would continue to be cherished and treated with love, honour, and respect. One bit of advice from him that I will never forget is: Always say less than necessary; once words are out, you cannot take them back. I have added to this: The more you say, the more common you appear and the less control you have. You are also more likely to say something foolish. Silence makes people uncomfortable, because they do not know what you are thinking. Short answers will put others on the defensive. They will jump in nervously and fill in the silence with valuable information, exposing their weakness. Robert Greene says in *The 48 Laws of Power*, 'Sometimes it is unwise to be silent. Silence arouses suspicion; therefore exercise it with caution.' I cannot repeat here all of my grandfather's intellect, but thinking about him always gives me the strength to move on, even at the lowest of times. May his soul rest in peace!

If he had been alive, however, I could not have gotten involved in politics. Not that he hated leadership, or service to others, but he was a strong believer in social stratification and respecting the lines therein. Politics would mean mixing with people of all social classes. He argued that if you invaded other people's space, you risked their invading yours, too. How true. To him, friends were good, but friendship was not to be exaggerated. Too much visiting was tantamount to loitering. He taught us that it was wrong to express too much emotion in public. We were not to cry too much or wail, even in bereavement, and were not to laugh too much, however happy we were, 'lest people looked through our open mouths into our stomachs'! My grandfather's metaphors meant a lot to me when I grew up. We were also to avoid loud and aggressive people and be careful with those who were easily excitable, as we might not be able to tell when they would come to us and when they would run away. It may sound confusing now, but because I heard these words from him over and over, in a way they influenced my character and helped me to define parameters within which to operate and beyond which I should not go.

CHAPTER 16

I was visiting my parents after more than a year of separation, the longest time I had ever been away from them. I had this strong and heavy news to deliver that was causing me anxiety; I did not know how to start. Unlike my children, who are free with me and I with them, I had never discussed with my parents matters of friends of the opposite sex—lovers, to be precise. It was taboo. When a former boyfriend that I had introduced to my uncle once visited home in Fort Portal, with his cousin who was visiting another friend in our home town, I had to go through a two-hour interrogation and lecture. Another time, the same boyfriend had written me a letter (thank God there are mobile phones now), using my Dad's post office address. My dad opened the letter and read it and did not even seal it again. He called me, raging, to ask why this young man said he loved me. Of course, I said I did not know! Parents now know that even children have the right to be respected. If you do not allow your children to be free with you, they will be forced to hide things from you. You will never know what your children do and will lose the opportunity to advise them appropriately.

I knew I had to compose myself and drop the bombshell. I had rehearsed the words, the posture, and the facial expressions in the mirror overnight, and had come up with the strategy of telling Akiiki first when we were in the kitchen; then she would advise me or be the one to tell Dad. I would execute the plan the following evening as we prepared dinner. I could almost guess the questions that would follow my admission: Where does he come from? who are his parents? How long have you known him?

What is the hurry? Mind you, I was twenty-four. I had all the answers ready; I could not wait to have this done with. The anxiety weighed so heavily on me, it was like a bag of cement on my shoulders. I wanted to feel lighter and very fast.

CHAPTER 17

Steven and I had dated for about eight months when I bumped into a friend, Alice, who knew us both and knew about our relationship. We had met her a number of times together before, or I had met her by myself and we had always had the usual general chat. This time she asked about Steven—she always did—but added something that took me totally by surprise. It was in reference to a former girlfriend of his, the one I knew casually. She said something to the effect that the girl had failed to get over Steven and accept facts as they were. I told Alice that we had met the girl once when we were together; she had greeted us and I did not think she had any ill feelings anymore, especially given that theirs had been a short-lived casual relationship which had ended a long time before. Alice, in a more matter-of-fact tone said, 'You know, Beatrice, if there were no children involved, maybe it would be easy for her to let go and forget, but …'. I did not hear the rest of the words. For a moment I thought I had not heard properly, or if I had, I had not understood. On the contrary, I had heard and understood. I felt my knees getting weak. I wanted to sit down, but I also wanted to throw up or go to the toilet, or both. Poor Alice did not know that what she had just said had been Steven's well guarded secret, and I, his fiancée, was hearing it for the first time. It took her by surprise when she realized that she had broken the most ridiculous piece of news, but the cat was out of the bag and it could not go back.

For about ten minutes, we were both silent. When she broke the silence she said, 'Beatrice, I am sorry.' Believe me, she was sorry because she thought he had told me about his children; she was also sorry for the casual way in which she had carelessly thrown in my face this sensitive piece of information. I was sorry too. Not for her, but for myself. It could not be possible, I told myself, but it was. It was not only possible, but true.

I had no energy to move. I was supposed to go back to work, but I wanted to know more, as much as I could before I decided what I was going to do next. Alice was working in a bank, but on Friday afternoons, most people did not go back to work. She had been coming from lunch when I bumped into her, but her handbag was still in the office. I begged her to stay with me longer so we could talk. She accepted, but had to get her bag. So I walked with her to her office, we got her bag and found a quiet place to sit and go through what she knew of the story of Steven, Maria, and the two children. It was not a pleasant story; it could not be for any woman, but to me, that was not the point. The point was that this man with whom I was in love, who had said he wanted to marry me, and who acted honest and straightforward, had two children and had not told me. I told Alice how I did not visit his house, because his mother, grandmother, sister, and brothers were all there. His mother had moved from the house she had been renting at a nearby estate on Naguru, which was not so secure at this time. She had all along lived with her own mother, so had moved to Steven's house with her mother, her daughter, and her sons—who were Steven's siblings. It made sense not to go to the crowded house. It was more peaceful and private when he came to my place. The few times we had together dropped food at his house after grocery shopping, he would call someone to pick up the food, and he would not invite me into the house. He talked to them often on the phone from my place, and I knew his entire family was in the house. It did not bother me at all. They say love is blind; it does not even have spectacles. I never thought too hard about this strange scenario. Besides, the few times I had met his mother, she was cold and had shown me no love. In fact, she could not hide her resentment, so I was not too eager to meet her often, either. In a way, I was scared of her. She had a sadness all over her, like someone who had missed a big piece of her youth, or had unfulfilled dreams. She seemed to mean more to her son that I thought she deserved, but it was not my place to comment. I was comfortable with the deception created purposely for me, that we should ignore her, and that whatever she thought or said did not matter. After we got married, Steven would go back for another course and I'd start studying for my master's in the United Kingdom. He had told me how stubborn his younger brother was and how at that age, he already had children who were also living with them at Steven's house. It all fitted in well, and I had no reason to doubt the stories or cause to cross-check this information. I knew the whole lot would find their level when we started our new family. I wish he had told me the truth. It would not have made a difference because I loved him and I knew too well that you could have a child or children with one woman but marry another. I would have taken those children and loved them the way Akiiiki loved me. It would be a God-given opportunity to pay back what I had gotten by offering it to someone else.

CHAPTER 18

God instead was giving me the opportunity to re-examine this relationship and most probably to quit. I did not take it. The explanation Steven gave me when I asked him was that he was too scared to mention it to me because he feared I might leave him. Also, his mother had advised him against telling me, saying some women even get to know about other children at the funeral of their husbands. This I got to know later, and wondered why she always gave the worst-case examples. The sad thing is, he took that advice.

I was very angry and disappointed. I wondered what else he had not told me, and how many more shocks lay in store for me. I could also tell that Steven was sorry and sad himself for having put our relationship in such jeopardy. He cried, begging for understanding and forgiveness. I did not know what to do. I grappled with the idea of quitting for about one week, but I never uttered a word. Meanwhile, he stayed with me as much as he could and even missed some days of work. He became warmer and seemingly more loving, but still part of me thought I was getting myself entangled in a web of things I might not be able to deal with. The children here were not my problem. The problem was that his mother had given him such bad advice on something that important—and he had taken that advice. Meanwhile, the mother of the children was spitting fire and bitter about having been mistreated by Steven's family to the extent that she was not allowed to see her children. This I was determined to reverse if I decide to stay in this relationship and get married to Steven. I believe that every parent has a right to see their children, and that, as much as possible, children should be protected from the bad side of their parents' relationship. I could see that most of my thoughts now were a subconscious justification of a decision I was about to make. I thought then that in every situation, however bad, there was a positive side. Sometimes we are too angry to see opportunities, or they may not be too obvious. In my situation, I focused on the opportunity—to prove to Steven that I was a very understanding person, and that in future, he should not fear to put things, however bad, on the table. Most importantly, I had the opportunity to address what I thought was a psychological problem for which I was convinced he needed not only forgiveness, but support and understanding. I underestimated the gravity of this matter, and put away, at least in my mind, how strange it felt and how much it hurt. Instead of dwelling on that, I decided that there was going to be some cleaning up to do. I was determined to give it a try and thought I might as well start right away.

I was conscious and deliberate, enjoying the upper hand over Steven and the higher moral ground on which this grave mistake had placed me. I assured him that we are human and that mistakes are part of our lives, but when we make them, we also have the responsibility to correct them and move on, being careful not to repeat them. So now, how was our life after marriage going to be? I had already decided I would take on and care for the kids. They would live with us as one family, and by that I meant just my husband, the kids, and me.

We had agreed that when the war was over, his mother, her mother, and his sister would go back to their house. His one brother (the other one was a teacher and rented his own house) could stay with us for a while. I later learnt that his mother had insisted she would take the kids, or at best give me the older one to test how able I was to look after a child. When the younger one was of age—I did not know what age, exactly—she could also come to stay with us, I guess if I passed the test with the older one. The reason was that I did not look capable of handling two kids, especially given that I did not have any myself. According to her, I might not even be intending to have children. I always wondered how one person could have this much crap in her head. It was like there was no more left for other people.

CHAPTER 19

I had earlier in life learnt the importance of mastering emotions but also detecting hostile grounds. If there was a way we could separate our family from my mother-in-law and define each other's territories, then there would be peace. What was clear was that this was going to be an uphill task. One bit of good news I'd got from our discussion was that we would be leaving for the UK for our studies soon after the wedding. Fair enough, I thought sincerely. I was getting uncomfortable with getting married to a man who depended on his mother's opinion on everything. I could not figure out how it would work. In spite of his continued assurance that everything would be all right, it didn't seem to fly.

PART IV

24th March, 2009 Bujumbura, Burundi. I've had a busy two days of meetings. Tomorrow, I have scheduled work for half a day, so I have decided to resume writing my book. The last time I wrote something was sometime last year. God, it is taking too long. Now I have decided I should be serious and finish it in the coming two months.

There are times when one feels that one should do what one thinks is best, no matter how many wise minds hold differing opinions. In such cases, it is better to be strong and wrong than a bit weak and right, though the consequences of either might be the same. I had a task ahead, and I had to accomplish it. The longer I waited, the more difficult it was going to become, because I had started forgetting some of what I had rehearsed overnight. This was a situation I should be in control of, no matter how hard it felt. I had to go through it—tonight.

CHAPTER 20

At 5:00 p.m., I followed my father to the farm where he normally supervised the milking of the cows for about two hours. We did this often, and it was something he, too, enjoyed, as he gave us information about which cow gave more milk—each of the girls at home had a cow named after her—and which cows had had calves, and we chatted as the herdsmen did the milking. I wanted to set the mood for a little later, when I'd break to him the news of my impending marriage. I had not told Akiiki yet, but still intended to tell her first, and make her part of my strategic planning.

After milking, I walked back to the house with my dad and went straight to the kitchen, where Akiiki was already supervising the preparation of dinner. I started the story and made it as brief as possible, ready to answer supplementary questions. The questions were not so many, I hoped my father would have only twice as many, but I knew he would have three or four times more, which would be followed by a long lecture. I was ready for a late night. Mum was understanding. She in fact said it was a pride to parents when a girl grew up with discipline, studied well, and found a man to start her own family. She was no surer than I how Dad was going to react, being the protective dad we all knew him to be. We agreed she'd tell him after dinner. Fortunately, if he was going to be tough on me, the agonizing period would be minimal, as I had already told him I was leaving to go back to Kampala the following morning. I would only go to say farewell to my grandfather in the morning before I left, having already visited my mother, who lived in another part of our district, and a few other relatives. I had no intention of telling anyone other than my mother, stepmother, and father until later. The other people that would know at that point were my aunties and uncles who lived in Kampala. I knew my father would be the one to tell those who lived nearer to home. That is, if he accepted and blessed the marriage.

CHAPTER 21

My heart started thumping when I heard Dad call me from the sitting room, but I steadied myself as I prayed for the session to be short. I did not expect it to be easy, but it was something I had to go through and had prepared for. It was like when a woman is pregnant and prepared for the inevitable pain because she is anxious to see her baby. I went and knelt on the floor beside the sofa where my father was sitting, opposite the one where Mum was. In our culture, you do not stand while talking to an elder who is sitting. Kneeling while greeting or when you are called is a tradition our home has kept. My father knelt to greet his father up to the time he passed away. In other homes, this tradition has been dropped in the name of modernization, as have many other courtesy actions. Globalization has not only affected economies, but has eroded our culture, too. Women dress like men, and men plait their hair like women and dye it to look younger. Some have sex with girls younger than their daughters or even with each other.

Anyway, I was down on my two knees. The silence seemed to last for an eternity. My father looked at me with such a disgusted face, as if he had nausea. You dare not stare straight in the face of an elder lest you be considered disrespectful, so I looked down to the floor and waited. I could hear his heavy breathing and the loud ticking of the wall clock. That look on his face was so familiar and it had long ceased to scare us because it had been overused—or probably misused, since it was applied to minor as well as major offences. In this case, I thought, it was being used for no offence at all. *Honestly, why is he making it so difficult?* I thought to myself. *What wrong have I done?* As I asked myself all these questions and gave myself the appropriate answers, he started. 'So you want to get married?'

I kept quiet for a while, because if I rushed I could land in a trap I would not be able to get out of. Quickly, I thought, *If I say yes, would it be he has no say, which would also mean I'm attempting to shake his usual authority to decide on everything for everyone?* I could not say no; it was not an option. I decided to play it safe and silly. I said I was considering getting married but needed his consent and blessing. Silence. I waited. Then the questions I'd been rehearsing over some days came almost in the same order I expected, and I gave the answers—short and precise—offering no more information than just the basics. Akiiki was quiet; she did not intervene and I knew she couldn't. It was some kind of unwritten rule that she'd managed so well. It worked for them both, but not for us children. He was the dominant partner, period. So we grew up hearing no quarrels between them. The gender equality thing had not yet been invented, and even when it was, they must have thought it was not for their generation. In fact, just last Christmas, my father was telling us a story about his nephew, who was going through a rough time in his marriage. What shocked and annoyed my father the most was that his nephew had asked the wife to leave and she had refused. Together with my brothers and their wives, we told him that the best thing this young man could do was to leave, because the time of chasing away wives was long gone. He argued with us that the house belonged to the man, and we explained that it belonged to the family, and that if his nephew became violent as he said he was threatening, the police would come and throw him out. His conclusion was that it was no wonder there were so many murders among couples. Maybe he was right.

CHAPTER 22

I had given as much information as I though I needed to about my husband-to-be, including that he was a mixture of two tribes, his mother being Tooro, which is our tribe, and his father being a Muganda. That made him a Muganda, my father emphasized, to which I answered in the affirmative. And then the difficult question came: Could I not find a Mutooro if I really want to get married? To this particular question, I kept quiet, although inside I answered by asking whether he thought women looked for men. Then the long lecture started. Apparently he saw no hurry. I was still young. He also knew that if I was patient, I'd get someone else from a family known to him. He ended by asking me to drop the whole idea and not see this man again. While inside, I was saying, 'You are joking, aren't you?', I just stared at him and did not talk. He ended by saying if I wanted to continue, I should know he would not be a party to it.

I stayed on my knees, because all that time he had not beckoned me to sit. I wanted to say something, but I did not know what. I kept quiet, remembering the canings they both used to give us, in most cases for no good reason. I also knew that my father loved me and that he'd been so tough on us because he demanded from us maximum discipline. Whether refusing to let me marry the man of my choice was part of this love and protection, I was not sure. Maybe it was just possessiveness. I now thought about Steven and his mother. I could understand her looking at me as a serious rival for the love of her first born son, probably more so, as she had had no husband. But she'd also invaded his space to the point of manipulation.

I made one more desperate attempt and this time asked, 'Dad is your word final?' He said it was. He got up and went to bed. I also got up and sat in the chair, and Akiiki now started. She reminded me how decisive my father sounded, and told me his first reaction when she told him was shock. She advised that I shouldn't go against his wishes. What a sudden change in her opinion! This was a bad start and I did not like it a bit.

When I went to bed that night, I went through the evenings's conversation. I was not convinced that my father had the right reasons for his decision. Inside, I was in a defiant mode, realizing that if things continued like this, it was going to be a stand-off. I had no idea how it would end, but I knew it had started. I respected my father and valued our relationship. I had tried my best to be a good child, but this time I was afraid all that might be trashed. In a way, I was scared.

The following day, I left for Kampla, and as he always did before we travelled, my father led a prayer for journey mercies. He also thanked God for having kept all of us safely during the war, for giving him good children who listened to and respected their parents, and he prayed to God that I would continue to be a good girl. It was all very well calculated.

I did not have to give Steven the whole story, so I was selective, the bottom line being that my father thought I was rushing. I concluded that I would give him time to absorb the news, and that I was sure I would get a go-ahead, sooner than later. Meanwhile, I started to write my dad a letter, which took me some days, because I'd write, cross things out, put them back, recompose sentences to make them milder, and read it over and over to ensure it did not sound rude. Patrick was going home the next week, and I wanted him to carry the letter. Finally, it was four foolscap pages, carefully written, answering some of the questions I'd feared to answer to his face. I enumerated so many marriages among same tribes that had not been successful, brought up many young men from 'good' families in Tooro who were a nuisance, and mentioned that as a girl I could not look for a man to marry. I ended by asking him to reconsider his position, and said that I had made up my mind. I was eager to look Patrick up when he returned, to get a reply. There was none. My father had not replied to my letter and did not for three months. I did not write another one; neither did I go back home to visit. I waited.

During the fourth month, he came to Kampala and I went to see him at my uncle's house, where he was staying. His cousin, Mr. Kagoro Victor, already knew about the situation, because his wife was related to Steven's grandmother. They talked well of Steven to my father, but he did not seem to be moved. He did not discuss it with me while in Kampala, but when he went back he rang and asked me to go and see him at home.

The following weekend I travelled to Fort Portal and spent two days at home. We talked and the mood was now different. He had changed his mind. He not only said I could go ahead, but he pledged all the support he could give, asking me to keep him in the picture with the arrangements and even proposed some people who could lead Steven's side for the formal introduction ceremony.

CHAPTER 23

My father is a very interesting person, though tough by all standards. Today when we tell our children some of the things he said or did, they cannot believe he is the same person, because he treats his grandchildren differently, and treats us now as equals, discussing and planning together. He loves us all so much and hurts if something concerning any of us does not go as he expects. In fact, he fusses over us so much so that sometimes we are forced to keep some little things from him to keep his blood pressure normal. Sometimes we wonder why he treats us like little kids, but now, as our own children grow, we realize a child will remain a child in the eyes of his or her parents. One lady in her seventies recently told me that parenting is a full-time job until one dies. Another very good Christian told me that no parent would enter the Kingdom of heaven, because parents want the best for their children, even at the expense of others' children. But all in all, children are a big blessing from God, and I believe he devised them for us to experience and exercise limitless love.

As he had promised, my father supported me all the way through the introduction ceremonies and the wedding. He gave a very good speech at the wedding reception, partly talking about me and what I had been like at home, with a lot of passion. Now I felt sad. My sadness had started the night before when I was alone in my bed; it continued when the church service started. The excitement I had felt briefly that morning had later turned into anxiety, but as we exchanged the vows as we had rehearsed them, I kept reflecting on them and wondering whether this lifetime commitment I was about to make would work—for me. I remembered the big lie, the difference between our families, and the strong hold over my soon-husband-to-be by his mother, who obviously disliked me. I was sure

I loved Steven, but not certain he would be strong enough to contain some of these contradictions for the sake of our marriage. I think I suffered from cognitive dissonance, which is an uncomfortable feeling caused by holding two contradictory ideas simultaneously. I was before a congregation and the Reverend was ready to administer the vows, and in no time, he declared us husband and wife. I felt a sigh of relief when he said, 'what God has put together, let no man put asunder'. It was over.

The rest of the day and evening was good, with the after-wedding-party going on until to the wee hours of Sunday, 18 January 1987. The few days of honeymoon that followed were even better. We were by ourselves, planning our future, and pledging total love and commitment, saying all the nice things.

CHAPTER 24

The new government was showing all the good signs of change for the better after only a year in power. President Museveni had formed an all-inclusive cabinet, which he called 'broad-based', taking on people from other fighting forces as well as previous regimes. The army was extremely disciplined and Ugandans were enjoying security and freedom that they had not experienced in about two decades. It was like Uganda had been reborn. The gloom that people had worn on their faces because of uncertainty on so many fronts was waning, expectations were very high, and people were ready to work. The government enjoyed a lot of good will from the people, and politically the masses moved together as one big 'movement'. This was the system of governance for twenty years, until multi-partism was reintroduced in Uganda. Even when it was, there was a lot of resistance, because of the history of abuse of power under the multi-party system. People did not distinguish between a system of governance and its key players, so they blamed both for past errors. The 'movement' system had allowed people to elect their leaders on a non-partisan basis, on individual merit, from down at the grassroots up to the national level. They were content with the arrangement, and I believe it worked during that time. A lot of healing had to be done if Uganda was to become cohesive. The political landscape had to change from the status quo, where politics had turned nasty, and tensions had erupted with time. The lid that had kept them closed up had flown off under a lot of pressure. The steam was visible.

CHAPTER 25

Shortly after my wedding, I got a job in government at the Ministry of Finance, in the Economic Affairs Department. Later I was seconded by the Ministry to the Directorate of Government Central Purchasing, which was going to be upgraded to a corporation with semi-autonomous status. The government had not yet embarked on economic reforms, which later decentralized procurement to the various government ministries and departments as well as local governments.

My time at the Ministry of Finance was a great learning experience that offered me exposure in government as well as outside the country. Being newly married, I was also going through a different kind of life experience.

When we got home to our house after the honeymoon, my husband's relatives, save for his sister and one brother, had left. After a short while, his sister also left, so it was the three of us and my house help, who had worked for me before I got married. My mother-in-law visited regularly, sometimes very early in the morning, This was something I found very strange. There was always something to complain about, or a not-so-friendly comment from her to my husband—but mostly to me. It was difficult for me to say how I felt, but what was confusing was that my husband never seemed to appreciate that there was some kind of rivalry here. I did not know the right thing to say, the right drink or food to offer, or how far to sit from her in her presence. I felt like a hostage in my own house. When she did not come to our house, my husband would go to hers. It was an unwritten rule that they had to check on each other almost daily; they were quite a pair no doubt. I wondered whether it was the same with all of her five children from different fathers, whom she boasted of having brought up by herself. I chose to ignore the trend; it was irritating but also in a way provocative. My marital space was being invaded—slowly and steadily. After only two months of marriage, I was being accused of not wanting (or not being able) to conceive. She said I had just got married to fulfil a goal in my life, but was not likely stay in the marriage. Looking back, I think people's bad words can be an omen.

The situation was not made easier by my husband pretending all was well and that I was fussing over nothing. Nothing, eh? The talk about going to the UK to study was never revisited, either by him or by me. There was no point. We clearly were here to stay, and I did not know whether the status quo would ever change or I'd live with this for the rest of my life—or hers. I decided it was best to concentrate on our love and close an eye to such distractions. I must admit it was a little difficult, as this man was clearly torn between two women he loved. I tried to be supportive, assuring him that the love for his mother was okay, that I loved him, that everything would be fine.

Meanwhile, I had conceived and was excited about the fact that I was expecting my first born. Not to prove anybody wrong, but I knew that was what should naturally come after getting married, and it had come. I don't remember my husband's reaction about this news; I had started accepting his indifference to things that would excite other people. I told myself engineers were meant to be serious people, but my father was one and he could get really happy and excited when something good happened. Steven was not happy at work and complained every day about one thing or one person. He believed there were many people that did not do their work, so he worked more; others did not like him because he was more qualified, so they undermined him. He thought he should have been promoted, but … and on and on. I became worried about him, because he was evidently unhappy. It affected me, too, because every evening was a complaining session. We could not therefore share my positive experiences at the Ministry of Finance. Steven dropped me off and picked me up from work; any delay in my coming down added to his frustration, and we would not talk for a few minutes. My husband changed—he became very moody—and I started feeling he was not as loving as he had been before. We stopped going out, my friends were clearly not welcome at home, and all of a sudden, my brothers were not good people. Ever since we met, we had gone together to pray at our Anglican Cathedral, All Saints Church. Without warning, he changed and started going with his mother to Pentecostal Churches. Since I was not invited, I continued going to my church. This caused a major shift from our Sunday programme, because their services went on for longer hours. I would get back home and have to wait for him to have lunch with me, until one Sunday, when I'd waited until 3:00 p.m., and then he came and said he'd eaten at his mum's place. Things seemed to be changing, and very fast, too. These might look like small little nothings, but collectively I started feeling their weight.

CHAPTER 26

In the Economic Affairs department at the Ministry of Finance, my immediate boss, Mr Odong Steven, had not recovered from the bug that had eaten into most of the civil servants during the previous regimes. He was never in his office. Even when he was there, he clearly had very little interest in the work. That was in a way a blessing for me, because I attended to most of his work and interacted with the permanent secretary, James Kakooza; the minister, Hon. C.W. Kiyonga, and his deputy Kafumbe Mukasa. One day I took advantage and approached Hon. C.W. Kiyonga, told him about my husband's unhappiness at the UEB, and asked the minister to help him get another job. The minister promised he'd get back to me shortly, after ascertaining where there was an opening for his profession.

I told Steven about this initiative and we hoped for the best. Steven himself had developed interest in the work that was going on at the Central Bank, where a new modern building was coming and they needed maintenance engineers. I informed the minister about this, and after he contacted the governor, Dr. Suleiman S. Kigundu, interviews were arranged and Steven got the job. We were both relieved that that problem had been solved. I hoped that now the stress levels would go down and the situation would also get better for me, because we had moved from the UEB house in Kololo, to a house farther from Naguru, where Steven's mother lived. I prayed we'd go some little distance further to reduce regular visits.

CHAPTER 27

A day after our first wedding anniversary, I delivered my beautiful daughter at seven in the morning. I had been in labour all night, with my mum—Akiiki—rubbing my back, giving me black tea, and explaining how, before I knew it, it would be over. I did not know when this hour or minute would come, but I could not wait to push the baby out; the labour pains were bad. In the ward where we were, my neighbour, who was taken to the labour room that night, lost her baby. Although I knew the lady, I wished they had not told me. It was so scary I did not know what to do. The more worried I became, the more the labour pains intensified, but the baby was not coming. I called the nurse after every ten minutes to check if I was ready, and each time she'd say, 'A few more minutes'. When the right time came, it was evident. I didn't even call the nurse, but ran myself to the labour room. I did not know what to do there, but shortly the nurse and my mum came and took me through the procedure. Within no time, my baby was out. I waited to hear the baby cry. It did, and then I asked whether it was a girl or a boy. I thanked God for giving me what I wanted.

I did not see my baby until later, after I was out of the labour room. My brother Patrick was outside the labour room as I went through the delivery, he was told as they handed him the baby, 'Your wife has had a healthy baby girl', whom he held happily. My husband had not come back to the hospital since he had checked on us the previous evening after I'd driven myself there earlier. I was with Mum, whom I'd asked to come and be with me after the doctor told me the tentative dates. Well, Steven came mid-morning with his mum, and a few other relatives came to see me. I was a mother; I cannot explain the pleasure, but it is deep, it makes you feel like a different person, and it instils in you an immediate feeling of abundant love, responsibility, and protection. I'd stare at the baby, trying to come to terms with the fact that this was my own, too good to be true. It was a normal and smooth delivery, and two days later I was discharged. I was not very sure, or I did not want to face the reality, but it occurred to me that my husband did not share my happiness. I thought maybe it was because he'd had children before, so it was nothing new and special to him. It took me aback in a way, but I again decided to ignore it. This was *my* baby, and I was happy whether the happiness was shared or not. Now I understood how women could most times withstand glaring failures in their husbands, because children provide an enormous source of comfort. There were no major failures to talk about here, but there was something not right though I could not put my finger on it. During my leave, I had some time to mentally turn the clock back, and saw for sure that Steven had changed. This was not the loving, mindful, considerate man I'd married a little more than a year before. I had been told that most men change, but I hadn't been told that it could also be so soon. After we solved the job issue, I had hoped the cause of his unhappiness had been tackled and the symptoms would disappear. They did for a while, but there were other symptoms now whose cause I did not know. I chose not to be emotionally drained by something I had absolutely no control over. I tried so much to please, but I guess I was not doing it right, as I did not see results.

CHAPTER 28

I went back to work after three months, but it was not easy. I had a young girl to take care of the baby, and I'd go a little late to the office, go back home to breastfeed at lunch time, and leave the office earlier. Thank God we were not sharing transport anymore. I used the family car while my husband had an office one. In the evening, if he wanted to go for his game of squash, I would be home so he would use our car. It all worked out well.

My sister Lillian, who comes after Patrick and Richard, had not done very well at her O Levels. My parents did not think she tried hard enough, but she did. It could have had something to do with an ailment she had suffered when she was about eight years old, which had left her with a slight limp in one leg and a twist in her left eye. I had got her a practical course at the YMCA in Kampala, and she lived with a maternal uncle and his wife in Kololo, Kampala. She had confided in me that she was not very happy there. I talked about it with Steven and we agreed she could come to stay with us. This, too, was a big relief, because Lillian went to school for only half a day, and it made me very comfortable knowing she was at home, because she loved the baby so much. In fact, Lillian brought up my babies together with me, and loved them and cared about them as much as I did. She witnessed a lot of my happiness as well as my sadness, and she shared it all with me. I made a promise and commitment to myself to stand by her and make her happy as long as I lived, and I thank God that I was able to fulfil it. Lillian completed her course and I got her a job. She worked for a while before I later took her to Nairobi for another course. She finished it and then decided to be self-employed. When I realized she was not doing so well, I sent her to the United States, where she has had better opportunities and made herself a better person. She made a difference in my life; I am happy I did the same in hers.

Sometimes I laughed at myself, engaging her in deep conversations, sharing my frustrations whenever I felt them and believe me, it was often. She witnessed us becoming indifferent to each other saw the constant anger and rage as the relationship fast deteriorated. If there was anything Lillian could do, I am sure she would have, but it was simply an affair of two people, and only the two could do something about it. All she could do was hurt with me and cry with me.

CHAPTER 29

Some people equate being possessive to being loving. I am not so sure about that, but whatever the case, when possessiveness turns into violence, I disagree with that equation totally. You cannot want to hurt the person you love, whether the hurting is psychological or physical. For me, deliberate hurting of others is an act of sadism if not outright hatred, and we all know that love and hate cannot occupy the same space. Even with my original cognitive dissonance, I refused, and I wish everybody could, to make excuses for violent behaviour. I know human beings try to rationalize instead of being rational beings when it comes to contradictory situations. It's cowardice, escapism, and deception. You end up living for others instead of yourself, and yet for your life to be worthwhile, you cannot live in fear, on hope, and be demeaned and robbed of self-esteem. Every life has forks in its road; sometimes the tines of that fork stab deep.

I was never sure what I was guilty of, but I found that I was forced to be on the defensive all the time. My husband and I became distant, and nothing could fill the empty space between us. I started feeling like I was under curfew in my own home. The first incident that was real physical left me feeling sad, worthless and rejected. It was after a visit to my uncle's house, a short walking distance from where we lived, and the problem was that I had "overstayed". Lillian run back to call Uncle Victor, whom I had visited. He and his wife came to find Steven also had left out of shame, but the harm was done and it was never to be the same again. Real life, unlike fairy tales, has more complicated endings—and beginnings. Lillian run back to call Uncle Victor, whom I had visited. He and his wife came to find Steven also had left out of shame, but the harm was done and it was never to be the same again. Real life, unlike fairy tales, has more complicated endings—and beginnings.

My mother-in-law later came in with her usual strange wisdom, telling me that my husband would be happier if I stopped working, which I refused outright. Then followed his apologies—something to the effect that he loved me so much he didn't want me to work, because he couldn't stand other men looking at me. I thought this was nonsensical, and if I started, I didn't know how far I'd go giving in. The battle of egos had started and the signs of failure were clear. How sure was I that an inch wouldn't turn into a mile? I was not going to change the fact that we were two individuals from different backgrounds who had fundamental differences. I realized that I'd remain sad and vulnerable unless these fundamental differences were bridged, or at least minimized, but I wasn't sure how they would be. I was anxious to rebuild and start again, but I could not do this alone—I was in it together with Steven, who for some reason had been swept by an inferiority complex it took me time to detect. We were not able to discuss issues that mattered to us; whenever we tried, it because more apparent that we were not communicating. The strain of having to calculate speech, weighing what to say and when or how far to go without causing harm by saying the wrong thing, was substantial, but nothing compared to the pain of what went unsaid.

I hoped for the best, but decided to prepare for the worst. In the event that this union collapsed, would I hang in there until it collapsed on my head? I had subconsciously started lowering the bar for standards, because life delivers far fewer disappointments when your expectations are low.

Evasta, my daughter, was only one year old. I had always prayed to God to give me four children. The way things were unfolding, I doubted this would happen. At the earliest, before things got worse, I wanted to have another baby in wedlock, and when the two grew up and got married, I'd have the four that I had asked God for. This was a dream that would linger for years. Meanwhile I had a plan to execute, and as the idea matured in my mind, so did the preparedness. It may sound crude, but I played it perfectly and deliberately conceived in February, 1989. I had my second baby in November of that same year, a boy. Everything else now did not really matter that much. There is the life you live and the life you leave behind.

CHAPTER 30

The situation did not seem to have gotten better or worse except that during the second pregnancy there was no physical violence, but a few acts and words now and then that were not really friendly. The good thing was that mentally, I had tuned my mind not to expect too much. I knew that when women are pregnant, some get pampered and others don't, and I had to live with the fact that I fell in the latter category. Surprisingly, I learnt from my own experience that you only lose what you cling to. Looking back, I am amazed at the amount of energy I had throughout that period, up to the logical end when, at 10:00 a.m. on 8 November 1989, I walked up the stairs of Mulago hospital, to floor six, straight into the labour room, and had my bouncing baby. I have always believed that the will of God will not take you where his grace will not protect you! That same mid-morning as I felt what I suspected to be labour pains, my Aunt Margaret came to my house for a totally different reason, so she was just in time to drive me to the hospital and help carry my pre-packed suitcase to the labour ward.

The baby had been overdue for almost two weeks, and boy, was he big! There was the joy of having had my second child—normal delivery, no hassle—and it was a boy. It's like the equation was near completion. Everything else that would follow, including if the marriage became normal again, would be a bonus. Not because I was a sceptic, but in life we need to know the basic minimums and avoid being too greedy; otherwise we risk losing what we have while we pursue what we think we should have. We might spend far too much time on the pursuit and expend so much energy, not knowing we are moving only in circles to go back where we started.

At the Central Bank where my husband worked was a new and very respectable secretary to the bank, Joshua Mugyenyi. My husband, too, respected and admired him and talked very well of him. Later in life, when I met and got to know his wife Mary, I lightly told her that my son had been named after her husband, but she did not believe it. I had accepted my husband's choice of the first name Joshua, but chose the last name that would reflect what I thought Joshua, my son, was to me—Muhumuza, or that who soothes, calms, consoles, comforts, and gives you peace and satisfaction.

In the Bible, Psalm 31, Joshua was a manifestation of protection from God. After the death of Moses, God gave him responsibility over the Israelites as they crossed the River Jordan to go to the promised land. In Psalms 1:5, the Lord says, 'No one will be able to stand up against you all the days of your life … I will never forsake you'. Joshua registered victory over Jericho, Ai, and five kings of Gibeon, as well as South and North of Canaan.

CHAPTER 31

When my own Joshua was about six or seven months old—and by that time I shared a bedroom with Joshua and his sister Eva, and not with his father—he suffered an attack of a disease that hit him suddenly in the middle of the night and left him almost dead. Up to today, I have never known what it was, as the doctors could not diagnose it. I was woken up by a strange noise from his cot and when I switched on the lights to check, Joshua was stiff and groaning, but not responding to me. I turned him and looked at his face, which looked lifeless. I was scared. I ran to the next room and woke up my kid sister Kate, who was at my house for holidays from school. I woke up the maid before I vigorously knocked on my husband's door. I was in panic. I held my son, with my sister beside me in the back seat and my husband at the steering wheel. None of us talked. I kept checking if he was breathing—he was, very lightly, but he was still stiff and his body temperature was alarmingly low. Steven had called the doctor as we set off from home, and by the time we arrived at the clinic the doctor was waiting. He was so kind, but that's not what I needed right then. I needed my child back to life, and after that, an explanation of what it was and what could have caused it. I was there to watch whatever tests were being done—the heart, the brain, malaria, epilepsy, and I don't know what else. The doctor could not hide his own helplessness, especially when Joshua did not respond as they pierced parts of his body with injections. We must have gotten to the hospital about 3:00 a.m. By 6:00 a.m., Joshua was not responding to anything. I had put my son to bed, bathed him, and fed him myself; he was okay when we all went to bed. His father also benefited from this information as I gave it to the doctor, because the rest of us went to bed before he had got home. He was probably hanging out with the boys, or the girls, or both; I would not know. These were issued I had conveniently set aside, to deal with slowly, steadily but surely, and at that time more than ever before, they did not even matter.

We were joined by another doctor at about 7:00 a.m. He listened to the story from his colleague as I kept my eyes on his face, watching his reactions and hoping for an answer, a solution. There was none. He did not even pretend to be academic, but he listened, looked at the results we had so far, and said nothing. This doctor moved to Joshua, checked the pulse, tried to open the eyes, and to our shock, gave the baby a hard slap on the cheek. I closed my eyes. After a while, my sister said something for the first time since we had left the house. She whispered that Joshua was turning his head. Then Steven told me, more loudly now, that Joshua was waking up. I also moved near, and saw how, like someone waking from a deep sleep, he slowly opened his eyes, looked blank for a while, and then smiled. Warmth slowly came back to his body. More tests were done, and I took him back two more times, but nothing was ever diagnosed. Joshua is now a healthy nineteen-year-old undergraduate, studying business finance and marketing in England.

PART V

You may not be able to change the past, but there is always an opportunity to change your future. One way of doing this is to discover what you are and what you want to live for. Mastering yourself is very important, if you are to live with purpose and fulfilment. A person's self-esteem is an ever-flowing reflection of what that person thinks about him- or herself on the inside and what that person does on the outside. What you share—especially with people that matter to you—is not how to bury your past, but how to write your future. Telling your story is one way to live forever.

CHAPTER 32

In 1990, as one of the economic reforms, the government procurements function was centralized—and later again decentralized. A Directorate was formed under the Ministry of Finance to handle all government purchases of goods and services. The government had identified and appointed Mr. Tim Lwanga—who had been in exile in Nairobi, working as a chief accountant in a private organization—as the Director General of the Directorate of Government Central Purchasing. There was a position of Procurement Manager, for which someone could be appointed from outside the Ministry of Finance where I still worked, or from within the Ministry on secondment. I thought about this opportunity, and though I did not have a procurement background, I knew I had worked hard and made my mark, and with my economics degree I could easily take a short course in procurement. I would surely apply the honestly and integrity that this job required. I chose not to share my ideas with my husband, because by that time, communication between us was almost non-existent. It was convenient for me to keep it at the bare minimum, because the violence had escalated to levels that were becoming unbearable for me. Our three and a half years of marriage had not been a waste, because I had my two beautiful children to show for it, but I was now sure that if I pushed it further, the rest would be a total waste. Steven was slowly robbing me of my self-esteem, and I was determined to regain it at any cost. My self-image was beginning to change; I felt worthless, incomplete, wrong. This affected me even physically. What was happening within me started reflecting on the outside. My smooth light skin was becoming dark and rough, I thought whoever looked at me twice could notice the battles that were going on inside me, and probably laughing. I tried to keep a smile, while telling stories to explain why I looked like that. Maybe people were not even bothered, it was just my own imagination, but there I was. It is a strain having to think of stories to explain this or that, eventually you run out. I was running out of stories and was getting worn out, partly by sleeplessness, to some extent by lack of appetite, but also by drinking. If I wanted to have a beer, I had to do it in secrecy because when my husband stopped drinking I too was meant to stop. I had not stopped, and this was one serious issue that had been tabled at a family meeting that was held to reconcile us some months back. The reconciliation was after a brief separation that saw me and my babies stay with my brothers for two months. Our getting back together was conditional on both sides. There had been so many dos and don'ts, promises and accusations, and fewer apologies. Some of the accusations, I was hearing for the first time, but I sat for three hours and went through it in front of my father, uncles, and in-laws. I felt humiliated, angry, and even lost, but only by admitting where we had failed could we take steps to do better the next time. Even at that meeting, I kept my thoughts to myself and my own words at the bare minimum as I watched my husband outdo himself with words that were potentially more damaging to our relationship, whatever it was going to be after that. His remarks were arrogant, and my father, being the wise man he is, internalized them and knew as well as I did, though he didn't say it then, that it was a matter of time and there would be no marriage.

CHAPTER 33

I got the letter of secondment to the Directorate of Central Purchasing and was to start work almost immediately. My terms of service had changed. I had a much better salary and was entitled to an office vehicle, a house and basic furniture, and medical and other smaller benefits. It was very exciting for me, and now that I was sure, I told my husband I was changing jobs. One of the reasons he had given for why I should stop working had been that the pay was too little to justify my leaving my toddlers with maids. Now I had an offer that matched his in terms of remuneration. This was another victory only I could understand; he probably understood it, too, but from a different angle. There are wars, besides the shooting ones, which, too, test mettle and resourcefulness and courage. But there are also some prisons with no bars.

I waited for the right opportunity to inform my husband about the new job and tell him that at the beginning of the month, in two weeks' time, I would start. He did not show much interest in the details, which suited me just fine. At least it was off my shoulders; I had informed him. I was particularly happy that I'd have my own transport to and from work, because before that, I sometimes had had to use taxis, especially coming back at lunchtime to check on the children. I will forever remain thankful to my friend Miriam Musisi, with whom I worked at the Ministry of Finance, whose personal car was always at my disposal whenever I had the need for one. If I wanted to do home shopping, run home to breastfeed, or take the babies to the doctor, Miriam's car was there for me. She was such an emotional support too, through talking and sharing advice, encouragement, and words of comfort. She never advised me to quit, but she tactfully told me stories that gave me hope of finding myself again—certainly not by staying in this abusive marriage. I know that this bad relationship was hindering me not only from being happy, but also from thinking straight. I also knew that if something is not good for you, it is better to let it go. It may hurt, but no more than it is already hurting. You cannot run away from the truth. There are so many things that would be great, if only they were possible, like if we could live life backwards from old age, feeling better every day, our illnesses disappearing, getting more hair, becoming more handsome, getting younger … mere fantasy!

CHAPTER 34

Working at the Directorate of Purchasing, which was outside the mainstream government ministries, was different. Though I liked the work, I had never liked the laid-back attitude the officers had at the Ministry. Reporting late, leaving early, dozing on desks, spending so much time on personal phone calls, and, in the offices next to mine in the department of taxation, discussing bribes and kickbacks as if it were part of the official work schedule. The new work environment was more serious, and I bonded with the people I worked with almost immediately. My boss Tim was strict, emphasizing discipline and expecting everybody to deliver within the given time lines. He was generally seen as arrogant and boastful, but I personally enjoyed a cordial relationship with him. Later in our lives, we shared a seat in Parliament and became very good friends, serving on the same Committee of Finance and Economic Planning. When my domestic tension intensified, I decided to share my problem with him as my senior but also as a respectable, happily married man. I was preparing him for the time when I would ask to take on one of my entitlements—a house—sooner rather than later. Tim showed a lot of concern, probably more so because he had five daughters. He was very categorical that he would not want to see his girls take any such nonsense. He had grown up in Fort Portal, my home town, where he went to the Nyakasura School, the same school I had studied from, and he knew my family. That in itself provided a strong connection, because Tim up to today is one of the old students who love that school and who hold the values that were instilled in us very seriously.

In the same office were two ladies who were close to me. Jennifer, the Legal Officer who later became the Corporate Secretary when the

Directorate transformed into a corporation, had separated from her husband, Dr. Muguma, and was going through a divorce. Louise was the Personal Secretary to the Director General and had been my friend for many years. Both of them knew part of my story about a failing marriage, and they went out of their way to offer me a shoulder to cry on whenever I wanted to, but also gave me a lot of encouragement. Louise, in particular, always insisted that I had a lot of potential and strongly believed that my potential was beyond what I was doing now. Louise and I have remained very close, almost like sisters. When she later got married, I was her choice to be Lady of Honour, but could not make it as I was travelling to Japan on an official Parliamentary Mission. We spent this last Christmas together with her husband Alex and daughter Erica at my house in Fort Portal, my home town, and we had a great time.

CHAPTER 35

The pleasure I felt starting a new, more challenging, better-paying job was shared by my friends, brothers, and sisters, while it widened the gap between my husband and me. I had never imagined that a man would feel such insecurity and envy because his wife was earning more and contributing to family expenses. I had long reduced my demands for household upkeep, but now that I could afford most of the things myself, it was a good excuse for him to pull out of the responsibility completely. I decided I would give my children the best I could, and this I have maintained up to today. I was continuously accused of all sorts of things, but mostly he accused me of infidelity. I had by now known that Steven was very possessive, had also got used to frequent accusations, including of infidelity, I got used to this, and I became indifferent even to getting back at me, which must have hurt, but why give someone the pleasure of hurting you? Clearly we were not intimate, we were no longer interested in each other in that sense. Like it or not, any sexual intimacy devoid of emotional connection never gives true satisfaction, but feels more like a chore than anything else. I was not prepared to massage his ego, something women do, hoping things will change things, praying it is a passing phase. During such a period, women are captives of pain, both physical and emotional, and most go through it silently, fearing to quit, hurting until they are laid to their final resting places. I was not going to share this conspiracy of silence with so many womenfolk. I would not blame myself, make excuses for him, keep up appearances, or even give flimsy reasons, like I was staying because of the children. My children would be better off brought up outside rather than inside this kind of environment, where they'd grow up thinking that quarrelling and fighting were the standard way of life. I had not experienced this with my parents, and I was not going to allow my children to. I had long lost the hope that things would change. Each day, week, or month showed more signs of the last phase of a dying marriage. No life-support machine would save it, but would only prolong the pain and agony. The time had come to turn my back on all this history, sign off on this chapter in my life, and move to a new direction— a direction where I would look at life in a more positive way, with an open mind, able to apply my full potential, without fear of being demeaned, intimidated, and embarrassed. Otherwise, I would soon become a shadow of my former self.

The children were growing, and my house help were so good, empathizing with me because they saw what I was going through. My job was good, and my brothers were understanding and supportive. We shielded my parents from most of the happenings because they'd hurt so much and I was planning my smooth exit. Under no circumstances would I leave the kids behind. At least I knew the law—because they were infants, and I was able and responsible enough to take care of them, I would not be forced to leave them.

CHAPTER 36

It happened faster than I had expected. The attitude I'd taken to ignore even the most provocative actions and comments must have given the wrong impression that I had accepted being a doormat. My mother-in-law surprisingly also held this false impression and would rebuke me to my face.

I returned from work one evening only to be told by my house boy through the fence that my husband had come home earlier and given instructions that if I ever came home after him, they should not open the gate for me. I let the office driver Lutaaya leave me outside the gate, as I did not want him to know there was any problem, lest I become the talk at work the following day. I insisted that the houseboy open for me, but the poor boy had no keys; Steven had them. The house boy, who had been our worker for a long time before I got married, was loyal to me and said if my husband let me in but beat me, this boy would this time hit him. The house boy said something to the effect that enough was enough, and that he himself had watched his mother being beaten day in, day out until she died of internal bleeding, leaving them behind to be later mistreated by a stepmother. What a scenario. I was outside the gate and my house boy was inside, crying for his dead mother and vowing to hit my husband if he dared touch me. I felt very sad that this was how far down I had gone, but I insisted that he attempt to ask and see if they'd let him open for me, but told him not to touch my husband even if he beat me. He came back after about twenty minutes; it was beginning to get dark now. I'd been there for about forty minutes. He told me that he knocked and told my husband from outside the bedroom door that I was at the gate, but he never answered and the house boy finally gave up. I asked him to position himself to receive shopping that I was carrying and was going to throw over the fence. I started to throw them one by one—packets of milk, sachets of juice, bread—some of them landing on the ground and breaking, and I was left with a packet of cereal when Steven came and talked to me from inside the gate. I don't remember his exact words, but it was a warning to the effect that if he opened, I would be dead meat. There was no point in answering, so I just walked away, up to the main road, and boarded a taxi to my sister Stella's house, which was not far from where we lived. Now as I write, it all comes back to me as if it were last week.

The rest is indeed history, but it is from history that tales are told. As luck would have it, Steven said he did not care if I took the children, playing into my hands and removing a hurdle I'd been anxious about whenever I thought about leaving. It was late February 1991. The following day, I went to see Sam Kibuka, Steven's cousin who was the best man at our weeding. Ironically I was asking him to come and witness me exit as he had witnessed my entry four years earlier. I could tell from the comments he made in his soft-spoken manner that in his heart, Sam wished he could make peace between us. He spoke of the children, patience, and forgiveness, not knowing that we had gone beyond that level, and that this was not the time to try the respect Steven had for him. When we got home, Steven was there, evidently ready to do what he had not been able to do the previous day. He must have been shocked at seeing me with Sam, and after a short exchange of niceties between them, Sam was but talking to himself. That day, I did not leave the babies and their maid behind. I took them with me to Stella's house, where we spent the night. The following afternoon, I went back, again with Sam, to collect my stuff and that of the children, as Steven had agreed.

CHAPTER 37

It's amazing how dynamic the world is. There is always another piece of news, however much moved we may be by one incident. A plane crash that kills two hundred people is sad and emotional, but if it happens in the middle of the Olympics, or the American presidential campaigns, it will quickly pass out of our attention. There will be a terrorist attack somewhere; the news focus will only last as long as there is no Tsunami or high-level political scandal. At a personal level, when one person is weeping, another is laughing for a different reason. While some mourn, others celebrate something at the same time, sometimes in the same geographical location. When one couple is quarrelling, another is making love, one is discussing not having a sixth child, another is seeing a doctor for fertility medication, and still another is planning their holiday or discussing family finances and choices for their son's university. Life is full of challenges and tremendous opportunities, and once you miss them, some come back and you have another chance, while others don't. All in all, the clock cannot be rewound. Life is not lived in reverse.

It's important to know that your world is not everybody's world, and that when your world stops, the rest of the world continues. People are always preoccupied with their own busy lives. If your car breaks down in the middle of the road, the drivers behind you will be impatiently hooting for you to give way, and if you're unable to move they will swerve, and drive by without even giving a second look in your direction. The mechanic who fixes it will expect you to pay before you drive the car off. Whether you have not yet paid school fees, have a close relative in ICU, or lost a job is all none of the mechanic's business. You have to keep moving. Sometimes you slow down, circumstantially or voluntarily, but you cannot stop, lest you cease to be part of the bigger world, and even when you do, it continues moving. Our small worlds, collectively, make up the bigger one, and yet each is too small to make an impact. Individually we cannot change the world, but we can contribute and make a difference.

CHAPTER 38

Moving on makes a big difference, and to a great extent it changed me emotionally and physically. My skin was regaining its colour, my mind was clearer, my delivery at work was better, and I am certain I became smart and beautiful. It was a whole new mindset; I knew I'd make it, and big time.

Rather than give undeserved prominence to that part of my life—a brief, failed marriage—I chose to focus on other things and avoided even discussing the details of what had transpired. That was my business and other people had theirs. Besides, I respected the institution of marriage but accepted that it did not work the same way for everybody, and that when it did not, the decisions were individual. I worked hard during the week and joined my brothers and friends on weekends for social gatherings. Sundays were for church with the children, except occasionally if I had a bad hangover. My younger sisters and brothers visited periodically from school, and we also visited them on their school visitation days. Free as I was, I maintained the responsibility of being a good mother to Eva and Joshua, a duty I am proud to say I have carried out successfully with my means. I was not scared of dating because of the bad experience, but was careful not to over-commit. In the event that someone came along and swept me off my feet—like a hurricane—I was definitely not going to have another child. My affairs were not to be public, although sometimes there's only so much one can do to hide. There's that human weakness when you relax, feel comfortable, and let go, but some instinct kept me in check. The society I lived in was small, so I could not be completely free of small talk. Sometimes it felt like everything was everybody's business. So I had to be cautious not to be part of everybody or allow everybody to be part of me lest I become a victim of mob justice or injustice.

CHAPTER 39

A year after my separation, my daughter turned four and started kindergarten. I was ready to start her on the new schedule of waking up early for school. She did so with a lot of zeal, which she has maintained. Eva had gone to school for two weeks when one day on reaching school to pick her up, I found her father outside the school gate. No one was allowed to pick a child except the known parent; if a parent sent someone else, that person would have an authorization letter and should have proper identification. I was very candid with Steven. I stopped and greeted him, careful not to express my surprise because we had not heard from him for one year. He had not seen the kids, and they had not asked about him. Joshua was only two now. I knew he'd come to see our daughter, so I asked him to wait a bit while I got her from class. I had to prepare my daughter, so I said, 'Daddy has come to see you. He's outside the gate.' Eva's reaction made me sad, but I kept a straight face and put on some kind of smile, held her hand, and led her to where the father was standing. After a short greeting, and Steven asking her about her brother and if she enjoyed school, we said bye and left. I did not think about it much, but I told my brothers and uncle. All of them expressed discomfort. In fact, my uncle advised me that I call Steven and politely propose that we work out a better arrangement than his coming to the school for him to see the children. I had not yet called him—I am not sure I was going to—when he turned up again at school three days later, on a Friday. He told me he'd take Eva with him and bring her back to school on Monday, to which I answered that since she had no clothes to change in, we should do it the following Friday. His response, 'You have continued to be stupid', surprised me, but I wasn't going to engage in verbal artillery. I decided I'd had enough of

90

that during the four years we lived together and was not going to waste my breath answering. Besides, it was a statement, not a question. So I said to Eva, who was holding my arm, 'Let's go.' As I turned to go to my car, where my friend Louise was sitting and watching us, I did not expect what followed; Steven gave me a hard slap on the face, which made me stumble, dropping my handbag to the ground. Without knowing, I screamed. Eva screamed too, as Steven landed me a blow, and I fell down. After a kick or two, he took off running with Eva while some parents who had witnessed the ordeal made noise, and two ladies who knew us very well came to get me off the ground, one saying, 'Beatrice, run after him and get back the child.'

I had to, and ran, with one shoe, and caught up with them before Eva was pushed into a vehicle where Steven's sister and grandmother sat, the poor old lady confused. I acted more quickly than the sister, because as he went around to the driver's side, I pulled my daughter away and she ran back towards our car where Louise was now outside, picking up my shoe, handbag, and whatever had fallen out. She held Eva and sat with her in the car. I had an opportunity to say what I wanted before he drove off because cars had parked very close to his both in front and behind. I told him that whatever happened when we lived together I had put behind me, but this one, he would not get away with it. I was too angry, too embarrassed and too confused to cry. Everything happened so fast.

Eva was so terrified that she refused to have her lunch. After dropping her at home, Louise and I went to the Central Police Station and filed a complaint of assault. The lieutenant and I went through all the necessary procedures—a medical examination, a broken watch as an exhibit. I made my statement and days later braved the court proceedings. I knew what I was doing. The ruling of the Court on this case was later helpful when I finally filed the petition for divorce. Two years later, I won the divorce case with proof of cruelty and adultery, because the woman he now lived with had had a baby and I had secretly secured the hospital records showing the names of the father and mother of the baby. He surprisingly tried to contest, but his grounds were flimsy. I had a responsible job, a steady income, and a sound mind, all of which earned me custody of the children. I wanted neither alimony nor maintenance, though my lawyer insisted he should pay school fees for his children, and this was put categorically in the divorce certificate. If I wanted to now, I could go back to court, using this certificate and file another case of failure to pay fees, but I know better than to squeeze water out of a stone.

PART VI

Greed by any other name will bear the same effects, just like a rose by any other name will smell as sweet. Human beings by their very nature will always want more, sometimes losing focus of what they already have, therefore failing to nurture what is theirs in a bid to chase what may never be theirs. Content, too, is relative. When it's looked at absolutely, it may manifest itself as laziness and complicacy, but it will always be better than vanity and bitterness.

CHAPTER 40

Evasta and Joshua are a joy of my life, a gift God gave me, a comfort at the hardest of times and a consolation when I think I am not quite achieving what I want. Both are at University in England, Eva doing Engineering and Joshua reading Business and Marketing. The three of us have a very strong and close relationship; we appreciate our differences and build on our similarities. I can boast of having brought up my children in a modest but loving way, instilling in them the important values that I am confident will push them to high levels in their lives. They are both very respectful of me and to other people, God fearing, transparent to a very large extent, considerate, and kind. Eva is very outgoing and more communicative than her brother, who takes his time with people and situations, but deep down is also a very good person. I know them both very well. There are situations when I have to deal with them differently, considering where each is more vulnerable.

The era we grew up in was different from the one in which I have brought up my children. While now we emphasize openness and sharing, it was not the same with our parents. With my children, it's like we stop at nothing. I have made them understand that no subject is too big or too sensitive to be discussed with a loving and supportive mum, who is exposed, well-travelled, and well-read, and has sacrificed a lot for their sake. Joshua is beginning to act like a man and keeps some things to himself until he's too happy, angry, or disappointed; then I come in. Eva has been consistent, and I have promised I'll be a part, even when she makes mistakes and errors of judgement—with her studies, friends, acquaintances, fears, and anxieties. She does not know that I keep more than twenty letters she wrote to me during her secondary school. Each of the letters was unique, but all of them were a pledge never to let me down and included her gratitude to God for having given her a mother like me. Every time I want to feel refreshed, I read them. My daughter is an above-average student; she has been an above-her-age child and is now growing to be a beautiful young lady who stands out from the crowd. Eva is a kind and considerate person who sometimes checks my excesses. One time, I complained that a worker was too slow, and she said, 'No, Mum. The problem is you; you are too fast.' She's more religious than Josh and I; these are not things I take for granted. I am always thankful to God for having given me these children and the ability to focus my life and guide them. I am neither complacent nor greedy.

At twenty-one and nineteen, Eva and Joshua have now mastered my 'sermons' that they call 'themes'. We have agreed that if you are to continue walking, you only have to look forward, not backward. This may seem obvious, but it is not. Some people lose their direction because they want to walk while looking backward. Few people have the determination to make each day better than the previous, or the sense to know that being in a place that's not yours is like posing for a picture to which you don't belong. I have seen people at a wedding join a photo for the bride, bridegroom, and parents when they are neither. I have seen those who take a reserved front seat until they are politely asked to move. People indulge in a little loose talk and spend so much time and energy on little nothings, leaving no energy for more important and bigger things. Thinking big but acting small can be a good strategy if well applied.

I have, therefore, shared with my children through illustration rather than 'do' and 'don't' orders. I emphasize that life should be purposeful; friends, unlike relatives, should be carefully chosen—they should add value to your life and should be good people. Bad people are those who are envious, jealous, rude, or liars and manipulators. But more important, take only what is yours to avoid enemies and sleepless nights. On a lighter note, we laugh about the small things in life and at people whose egos are too inflated as well as those who have none. They tease me about a boyfriend and ask about the possibility of my remarrying or having another child. I am happy to have these two wonderful people in my life.

CHAPTER 41

Kigali, Rwanda, 4 November 2009. I have just finished reading a book that was written over a period of six months. Mine is well beyond four years. I must have a story to tell. I am taking so long out of either laziness or disinterest, or I am too busy to really focus my mind on this book. For my own comfort, I want to believe it's the latter—so be it.

I have actually been very busy traversing the East African region for one meeting or another, conferences, or other events. I am very happy with the job I am doing at the East African Community (EAC), serving as Deputy Secretary General in charge of the Political Federation. It's not at all easy, with the EAC being an intergovernmental organization of the five sovereign countries of Kenya, Tanzania, Uganda, Rwanda, and Burundi. They have agreed to integrate, through four broad but interrelated states, a Customs Union, a Common Market, a Monetary Union, and finally a Political Federation. That is the order of the process, and my specific docket is the final and ultimate goal. It is challenging because I practically oversee the whole process, to ensure that it's on schedule and on course. I've also realized the need to make this integration process very firm, so that each stage we finish is irreversible. I have been saying in my sensitization meetings with different stakeholders that the EAC will be like Jesus; he died once and was resurrected and will never die again. The EAC integration started and progressed very well in the 1960s and 70s, collapsed in 1977, and was revived twenty years later.

The Summit of Heads of State is scheduled for the week after next. It will be preceded by the Council of Ministers. Besides the landmark signing of the Common Market Protocol, it will be a big celebration of the Tenth

Anniversary of the EAC; 1999 was when the Treaty was signed. This was a second attempt following the first where so much had been achieved: a common services organization, which established the East African Railways and Harbours, the East African Post and Telecommunications, East African Airways, East African Development Bank, the Examinations Board, Currency Board, and many other institutions. For my part I expect the Summit to give guidance on a road map towards Political Federation. I have spearheaded a lot of initiatives to lay the foundation for the East African Political Federation (EAPF). My specific area is covered under Article 23 of the Treaty for the Establishment of the EAC: Political Affairs, Foreign Policy, Peace, Security, and Defence. Each of the Deputies Secretary General (DSG) at the EAC is charged with a specific docket. The term for a DSG is three years, renewable once, and my second term began this year in May, so I have two and a half years left and I am determined to make a difference in EAC. I love my job and the challenges that come with it. Sometimes it gets very tough and I get tired. Thank God I have no young children at home or a husband demanding attention and time. In a way, this job fills the gaps, although I have to make time for the children during holidays and for my boy friend (or is it man-friend) whenever we plan to be together.

The things that I would like to see happen include Partner States agreeing on the structures in the EAPF. These would be defined in the East African constitution, as they would no doubt impact on the administrative structures existing in the five countries. I am in the process of working on the protocol on Good Governance which includes four major pillars: The rule of law and access to justice; democracy and the democratization process; human rights and equal opportunities; anti-corruption, ethics, and integrity. The draft has a protocol also providing separation of powers. The Peace and Security Protocol is pending signature, though activities are ongoing, to address cross-border crime in the Common Market, where there will be free movement of goods and free movement of persons and labour. We have developed a strategy to address non-proliferation of small arms and light weapons, anti-terrorism, and cattle rustling. Most important under the Peace and Security protocol will be the Conflict Prevention, Management, and Resolution (CPMR) framework, which attempts to create structures to address those aspects. All programmes related to conflict in this region, and indeed on the African Continent, have been more for the 'management' and 'resolution'. It's high time we addressed the 'prevention'. A Conflict Early Warning Mechanism has already been endorsed, and under this, we'll look at various sources of conflicts, including political issues like electoral processes, human rights, corruption, economic issues—fights over natural resources, environment issues, land, distribution of wealth, and many more. We will address social issues, including discrimination against some sections of people, like women, youth, the elderly, and the disabled, issues of culture, and access to education and health.

The integration process has brought out some fears and concerns, but where there's a will, there's a way. The Treaty requires the Partner States to harmonize their foreign policy, but they instead have chosen to harmonize the coordination of their various foreign policies. I guess as we go along, enough confidence will be built and the Partner States will appreciate more the need and necessity to give in more.

I would also like to see the defence cooperation go beyond mere joint training, sports, and cultural events to a common defence mechanism. A standby force to protect the bigger economic region from internal as well as external peace-disrupting tendencies. This is one sector that has been exemplary, but more can still be done. Our armies need to start looking at themselves in the context of the ultimate goal of one country called East Africa.

CHAPTER 42

I admit, I like my present job, but it has in a way directed me from my first area of specialization—economics. I am not very far from the second area in which I got my masters—public policy and management—and I am right in the middle of what I practiced for ten years before I took on this job—practical politics—but at a totally different level and therefore with a different perspective now—a wider one.

I also enjoyed what I did previously, especially in Parliament, where I decided right from the beginning to concentrate on my area of competence. I talked to a few colleagues and warned them against being Jacks of all trades, but many thought otherwise. Sometimes it is important to have something specific attributed to your name. Certainly being a Member of Parliament should not necessarily make you an expert on everything: the environment, agriculture, primary health, HIV/AIDS, energy conservation, power generation and distribution, fiscal and monetary policies, monarchism, domestic violence and/or female genital mutilation. But alas, elected people's representatives are sometimes know-it-alls who, in the long run, out-work themselves taking over everything without much in the way of results. When I decided to quit active (or elective) politics in 2006, my colleagues were offended by my frank admission that I did not feel intellectually challenged by Parliament anymore. I was talking for myself and from my heart. I wanted very much to respect my colleagues and the institution I had served for ten years. I looked back at what I had done with pride and satisfaction. What I was saying, simply, was let me move on before I become irrelevant. I had chaired the Finance and Planning Committee for the last three years of my first term, and then the Budget Committee for the five years of my second term. I had now found the opportunity to link my economies with my politics for improvement of social economic development. I had also had quite an incredible opponent in the previous elections in 2001, a lady who was abusive and disrespectful of me and other people, and who talked very ill of my parents. I did not have the nerve to go through that ever again, either.

I had joined Parliament in 1996 through a by-election following the appointment of my predecessor, a very good friend (now Uganda's High Commissioner to the United Kingdom), Joan Rwabyomere, to the External Security Organization as Deputy Secretary General. She had served on the National Resistance Council—a transitional party—the first year after the liberation war, and also in the Consultative Assembly, which debated the 1995 Uganda Constitution. In that first attempt, I was unopposed, so I had not really gone through the dirt most people associate with politics. I was satisfied with my performance both in my Constituency and at the national level. I believe many people, too, were satisfied. I really liked serving the people; what I did not like was to do it 'at any cost'. I wanted to retain some dignity. More importantly, my children had with time grown to hate my being in politics; they felt we no longer had quality time together, and probably no privacy. One morning in the constituency, three early guests were offered tea and bread, but made themselves too comfortable at the dining table and ate the children's eggs and sausages. That was not funny! I saw the exchange of glances between Eva and Joshua, and their cousins Patricia and Comfort, who were with us. They could not prepare more for themselves because there were no eggs and sausages left. The children hated, maybe more than I did, the campaign period I went through in 2001. They could never understand how anyone could be so abusive to their mother. After all was over with the campaigns and we were sworn in as members of the Seventh Parliament, my children and I had a long talk, at the end of which I promised to never again subject myself to the demeaning exercise. Little did they know that I had made that decision long before, in the middle of the campaign. I shared this decision with a few other close people, some of whom thought it was a reaction that would change with time because of their belief that politics is addictive. Maybe it is, but the addiction fortunately did not catch with me. I had had enough time now in which to plan a different path for my life.

CHAPTER 43

In 2001, I made up my mind to pursue further studies and started applying for masters' programmes in some Universities abroad. I was bent on going to a good University, and in 2003 after satisfying all the requirements and passing the admissions exams, I was admitted to the Kennedy School of Government at Harvard University. I could not have asked for more, but I looked at the cost involved and thought it was quite prohibitive, at least for me at that time. All the same, I readily accepted the offer and went ahead to apply for the available scholarships for that course, which Harvard had included in their information package. One that I chose to pursue was the Joint Japanese/World Bank Scholarship Programme, which was highly competitive but could cover about 70% of the financial requirement for the course. Fortunately, I had had some dealings with the World Bank during the time when I chaired the Parliament and Budget Committee and in the previous Parliament when I had chaired the Committee on Finance and Economic Planning. I had also done some consultancy work for the World Bank. To qualify, one had to pass through a process of writing essays and research papers on topical issues. It was easy for me to choose the topics that I knew would impress the World Bank; I knew where its focus was. For some reason, I was confident, which helped me to do my things slowly and steadily but also keep them to myself except for one person with whom I had a different relationship from the one I enjoyed with my several male friends. He was extremely supportive at every stage, including reading through some of my essays and going through all the University documents to ensure I had not missed anything. He knew how badly I needed to do this and how determined I was to move on and away from politics. I refused to discuss any plan B in case the funding didn't come through. In my mind, that was not an option.

In May 2003 I received confirmation of my scholarship and additional funding from the Mason Fellowship reserved for mid-careers in developing countries. This is what I had been praying for and could not ask for more. It was now only a month before the course would commence. I started panicking. My mind had been so preoccupied with the admissions process and looking for scholarships that I had not focused on some pertinent issues. In order of importance, they now started coming. Who would take care of my children? Though they were both in boarding schools, they would have holiday breaks. I had a five-year Parliamentary term with three years remaining, I was chairing a very important committee, and I had a constituency. Hard decisions had to be made here; I decided to tackle the issues in reverse order. I would not tell my constituents, and by the time they found out, I'd probably be halfway through my course. I had gotten the constituents used to my regular visits and close supervision of the development projects I had started for women. This was actually the smallest of the issues, because I was not going to answer any questions, or give my voters an opportunity to make this a campaign issue, since whatever it was that I would do after 2006, it would not require their mandate. Cool. The Committee: I would inform my members and request my vice chairperson, Hon. James Mwandha, to decide if he would stand in for me or take over as chair altogether. It was not personal property, and though I really enjoyed the challenges of the work I was doing, I could only chair that Committee for as long as I was an MP, but here I was, planning my exit. Brilliant. As a serving MP, I need not go away stealthy. I would inform the Speaker and ask for a few months' leave of absence. I would keep coming back whenever I could until I finished my course. Done. Now the children.

Joshua had only joined secondary boarding school that year, and he was taking time to adjust to being away from Mummy. Eva was in her third year, and still cried each time I dropped her at school for a new term. They had always lived with me, and when I travelled upcountry or abroad, which I did very often, I'd get a sister or cousin to stay with them, but they knew I'd be back in a few days. I had options worked out in my head, but I decided they should take part in the final decision. I had always attempted to be democratic in the house, but they were also aware that sometimes I practiced 'guided democracy', which is not quite the same as high-handedness. I know which one of the options they were likely to take, and before I discussed it with them, I went to my Uncle Robert's house and broached the subject with his wife Doreen, who readily and with pleasure agreed to take care of the children, even before consulting her husband.

The following weekend, Joshua had half-term break, so I picked him up and drove with him to Eva's school, where I'd sought the Head Mistress's permission to see her since it was not an official visiting day. It was an emotional time as we discussed the options for where they would go for the holidays, including their dad's, my brothers', my sister's, and my uncle's places. We hugged and wept, but also prayed. It was a trying moment for me, and I felt sad. After this hurdle I would go to see my parents and would be all set to leave. Days were running out fast, and the weekend before I left for the United States to start studies with the summer programme on 14 June, I threw a boat-cruise party for about seventy very well-selected friends, who only then learnt of my going away, when I gave a very short speech on the boat in Lake Victoria.

CHAPTER 44

I have many acquaintances. Those that I choose to call friends are friends in the true sense of the word. I have the habit of dealing with friends separately, and unless it's extremely necessary to bring them together, I keep them in the various compartments where I have placed them. In fact, I don't understand people who describe every other person they greet or laugh with as a 'friend', and I don't understand keeping in big groups of people, some not exactly compatible with each other. My friends, therefore, do not have to be each others' friends, and enemies of my friends are not automatically my enemies. This is probably also because I am not very good at making enemies. I'd rather run, even if I don't come back, than make enemies. It might be a weakness, but who doesn't have weaknesses?

I like to keep my friends, and as much as possible, to keep them happy. I do not have many friends I call close friends, but I have some simple standards of what is required—no, expected—of a friend, so that they do not get emotionally exhausted and overworked by the friendship. I, like everyone else, have faults and flaws, but I will stick with friends, protect them, and treat them with warmth and generosity, making each of them feel special. People need not really know to which compartment in my life they belong. In the 'inner' circle, there are only a few, and there are those that I'd rather not get too close to, especially those I sense that have a high capacity to let me down. On my side, I try not to overstep the mark, saying what I should and being careful not to abuse closeness. I do not believe that friendship should be totally unconditional and non-judgemental, so I let a few people know the private me—my fears, anxieties, success, and failures. I allow them to comment, criticize and advise. What I cannot abide is not being told the truth, however hurtful; it comes down to abuse of trust. A small white lie could very easily end an association, as would a wicked sense of humour because I hate malice, mockery, or cynicism. I do not like keeping up appearances, it consumes a lot of energy, which could be used for more valuable things. More often than not, liars start believing in their own deceptions, believing they are what they are not. Such people can never be genuine friends, because since they cannot stand their real selves, they cannot have true personalities or true feelings.

To me, compassion comes naturally, even to people who are not friends as such. I can confidently say it's an intrinsic part of my nature, which those who know me have experienced on many occasions. I have a character that many people are unable to describe—tough but also soft, strict but accommodative, fast but patient. Sometimes even my close friends will not know which one I will pull off. When I lose temper with people who are too loud or too slow, I quickly remember that we're all different and collectively, with all our differences, we make the world.

Compassion can manifest itself in many ways, but any of these can make a difference in people's lives. You can bring calm, reassurance, and hope with only words and gestures. To me, a smile on the face of someone in distress makes a difference. It's like light at the darkest of moments. A few bucks, which might be loose change to one person, could mean a meal for another. Those old clothes stuck in our wardrobes and out-of-date fashions in our trunks could dress ten poor and naked people. There is so much we can give or do for other people in this world, but we are all preoccupied with our own busy schedules in a fast moving world. My friends know what I think about vain, proud, and arrogant people. I cannot stand show-offs. But, again, who of us does not have weaknesses? They just vary in intensity, but for me they help to decide exactly in which compartment to place someone.

CHAPTER 45

Friendships are much easier to deal with than love affairs. The two types of relationships are sometimes treated exclusively of each other, seen as complimentary or even supplementary. The benchmarks seem to be different, with different people. What is common, though, is that everyone tries to put the bar for love relationships so high and then with time relax them, adjusting downwards and trying to justify each stage of adjustment. Could this be explained by the yearning of everyone to be loved? Isn't it amazing how much has been written or read about this subject, some of it so contradictory, by people who claim to know more about it than others. When the going gets tough and we are trying to hang in there, we may hear things like love is blind or love is patient, kind, does not keep a record of the wrongs, and so on. The tendency is to try to make it an entity on its own, an object, separated from the human being who is experiencing that love. Many things, of course, are easier said than done. Most times, they are not even discussed, or if they get discussed, half- or quarter-truths are told.

In the world of love affairs, people say many things they would not do, even if they wished they could. There are situations where quitting is as hard as staying. Each person should be left to use his or her own judgement. Besides, what one calls love another does not! A uniform definition is just another illusion.

When I asked one lady if she was still in love with a man, she answered, 'Love, umm, yes. I see him once in a while, we still sleep together, and he still pays Amanda's fees.' Amanda was her daughter, not his, and it might sound like a materialistic relationship, but I guess they each got their share of the pie. You might be quick to pass judgement that this is not love, as I did myself, but who are we to make that decision? One man thought a lady was so much in love with him because she praised him all the time, telling him he was very smart, had the best smile, and made wonderful love, and she would die without him. Maybe she meant every word, but who does not know that men have egos that they love someone to keep massaging? In this case, only she would know whether she really loved him or not, but if it comes down to what was in it for both of them, again, isn't it a draw? So, say the right words, do the right things, make everyone happy, and live happily for as long as it lasts.

Confusion might arise between infatuation, love, sexual relationships, flings, and so forth, but if it comforts people and makes them happy to call it love because they like what they are doing, why not? What's the point of calling terrible people beautiful names? Isn't it like beautiful prose in an ugly world?

Let's agree that when it comes to love affairs, common standards may not apply. They are so individual that there's no point even discussing the subject, because it makes no difference. You will not convince someone who thinks he/she is in love that it's not love. The benchmarks are different, the bottom line is individual, and evaluation is complicated, because the variables keep changing, rationality is compromised, and sadly, the auditor is also the accounting officer—it's a pure conflict of interest. One very good friend of mine—male—once warned me against intellectualizing on this subject. He said I run the risk of not enjoying these relationships if I read too much into everything. The alternative? Relax, let go, sit back, and enjoy it—especially when you are not young anymore, or have given up hoping for a life-long partner. But even if you are not young, it does not mean 'anything goes'. As another friend says, 'Only ensure a few basics are right.'

CHAPTER 46

The time I spent at Harvard was quite enriching in so many ways. It gave me time and space to refocus and take stock of my own life, from so many angles. I looked at society and how collectively we influence its direction of thought and actions; governments, their policies, and how they could do better; global economic and political power dynamics and how differently they affect the different continents, but also the regions therein; international institutions and what more they could do to make a greater impact.

I interacted with mid-career professionals from Bhuttan, Mexico, Oman, Singapore, Qatar, Australia, Norway, Nigeria, Macedonia, Jamaica, Ghana, Bangladesh, India, Kenya, Peru, China, Palestine, Germany, Sweden, Israel, the United States, and more. We were such a collection. We have now created our own alumni network of the KSG Class of 2004, keeping everyone informed of where each of us is, what we are doing, and where we are travelling, so that colleagues in that part of the world can meet up with us. The class members I meet more often are Kathy from Rwanda, Wanja from Kenya, and Sameer from India, now working in New York. Sameer is intelligent and funny, but very provocative. He always stirs up our debates on topical issues by making controversial statements, and he is very intelligent.

The KSG gives you that feeling that you could do it better. It's therefore no wonder that when about fifteen of us recently met during the UN General Assembly and treated ourselves to dinner at a nice restaurant in downtown New York, a third of my colleagues had political ambitions targeting the highest offices in their countries. You get so much knowledge, in a manner that's simple, but you are also made to think through it in a way that opens up options, each with its pros and cons. It's such a beautiful feeling, but not for the faint-hearted, because you can also feel bitter about what could be done and is not done, or wonder why people choose the wrong options when there are so many right ones. You may even think that governments use myopic people to implement good policies, or brilliant people who implement myopic policies, or both. It's also energizing to feel that if you got the opportunity, you could make positive changes, and very fast, too, until you realize that that opportunity can only be given by someone. No wonder my colleagues think they should now take the highest executive power in their countries. It's amazing how much each of us can do individually or collectively with others to change the societies we live in. It's even truer when we detach ourselves from the environment we live in and the expectation that someone somewhere will make things happen. The expectation that someone else should do it, not really accepting that it's what each of us does that makes the whole.

Classes at Harvard focused on public policy—economic, social, and political—avoiding, I guess deliberately, being descriptive, so the students' minds are tickled into deep thinking. Clearly, there was an attempt to expose us to and study the different schools of thought over certain policies without openly saying that the international development institutions were revisiting some of the prescriptions they had made for less developed countries over the years. Transformative ambitions had not produced the desired incremental positive changes. The big bang approach that could probably have had drastic changes was to some extent said to be looked at suspiciously by politicians, because that approach, too, had possible negative repercussions. We discussed the effects of policies that had been a result of snap judgements, avoiding long consultative deliberations, and whether one size fits all. In my country, for example, I argued that though privatization was not a bad policy per se, because Public Enterprises (PEs) drained the treasury due to mismanagement, subsidies, and wages for the numerous employees who did not match output, there had been no back-up plan for job creation. The government cannot completely avoid its responsibility to provide basic infrastructure and development, deliberate policies that would give a big push to the private sector.

A huge grid cannot be an engine of growth unless there's a whole new network of national transmission lines. Decentralizing without sources of revenue at lower levels would increase dependence on government and pressure for creation of more units, all creating more regulation and increasing corruption. Increasing enrolment for primary education without addressing teachers' numbers, quality, and remuneration, leave alone enhancing the inspection function, would not produce sustainable, visible progress. Plans, I know very well, are based on resources we need, not the resources we have, and yet my country for a long time was an example of the success stories of reform. A lot has been achieved, more can be done, and we should not stop thinking because we have the responsibility not to stop.

PART VII

March 10th, 2010: Bamako, Mali, Olympe Hotel. This is where I started writing Making a Difference *five years ago, and I will deliberately end it here by beginning on the last part. It is by sheer coincidence that I have found myself in Bamako—my destination is Dakar, Senegal, but on landing here in transit, the plane was found to have developed a mechanical fault and could not proceed. Hopefully, we will leave tomorrow, and then I will be able to catch up with my meeting, organized by the African Governance Institute to discuss the 'New Thinking for African Developmental Governance'. I will present a paper on the EAC Good Governance Framework and how governance issues are being shaped to contribute to our regional integration process. The subject may not sound so romantic. In fact it is very sensitive, but I think it may open our minds to think about what it is that has been missing in all the attempts towards development in most poor countries. With all the reforms, the money that donors have pumped into Least Developed Countries, the improved levels of economic growth, surely something is not right somewhere.*

CHAPTER 47

I have encountered a problem lately, I don't know if it is new, if I have just all of a sudden become aware of it, if I am more sensitive, or if the world is generally changing. I am meeting more people with characters I could call inconsistent or deceptive, who suddenly change the tone to suit situations. I cannot at any given time determine whether, indeed, their outlooks or mindsets have changed. These are people in responsible positions who go around the truth or tell open lies. I have seen those who nod in appreciation during a speech or a talk only to get out and trash everything. I can understand suppressing strong opinions for the sake of quickly concluding an unserious or inconsequential conversation, but I cannot understand deliberately denying people information, or twisting it to reflect something different from the reality. Others genuinely have perceived fears borne out of wild imaginations, so they end up failing to deal with substance and waste a lot of energy on form. Probably, some feel that their existence is threatened, and here I need not be judgemental.

The effect on me is not exactly negative; such are things that make people adjust to being more open-minded, patient, and tolerant, but in my case, also more analytical and less intuitive and emotional. Maybe this is what diplomacy is all about. Toe a middle and safe ground , be less technocratic without seeming remote, accept you are part of a crowd that may need or expect more from you than you can provide. You may also occasionally need the crowd to roar and applaud you, probably for validation, so try to connect with them emotionally. Confusing, isn't it? But connecting with the crowd is a perfect political tool, except we should remember, much as we want to be politically correct, not to be lured from making decisions that are responsible and responsive.

Know that in the crowd, people have an unprecedented freedom of choice, but as long as the crowd has been moved in a certain direction, if it is in your favour, you may as well keep your opinions to yourself. This analogy might help me to desist from lumping people into a stereotype and dismissing them. We may hold different views—miles apart—but remain small components of the whole. We can form opinions about people without necessarily hating them, lest we lose our own ground. But also, if we do not listen to others, they will not listen to us, so our good ideas and intentions will not make a difference. Even when we have detected untruths, shouting matches will yield no results, as in most cases, there are no winners. If you are more careful and patient, you might also identify some good people, and a few who are simply sleepwalking through many of life's sliding doors. They may be trying to fit their small dreams into your big world, or aiming at the middle, not the top. They all go through those same doors.

As I approach fifty, I realize that I have had more and more to bend backwards to accommodate certain situations, especially those over which I have no control. Life cannot be lived in a straight-line, rigid kind of way. Compromises are often made, but as long as you remain within the precincts of the values and beliefs you hold dear, the rest are details. Sometimes, that is where the devil is, in the details. There are those basic things that make you what you are, distinguishing you from other people. What you really are, and not what you want people to think you are, or what you would wish to be. Those you should maintain if you do not want to lose yourself. Like everyone else, my outlook has been influenced by happenings, but more so by people—those I love, acquaintances, a few I tolerate, and even fewer whose paths I pray will not cross mine, unless it is unavoidable. The number of people I am able to influence is likely to continue to reduce for many reasons, one being that I have tremendously cut down on associations. I want to feel myself.

One important belief I hold is that no amount of time or loneliness will affect my relationship with God. For most people, this relationship varies between indifference, neutral, and extreme. You know, like low, medium, high? I do not subscribe to religious fanaticism, or any other for that matter, but I firmly believe in God and the fact that we cannot escape him, even when we attempt to refuse him. He resurfaces somewhere else. The misguided sense of worldly enjoyment sometimes makes us lose focus of spiritual enlightenment, forgetting that the boat of life is constructed in such a way that it must move to only one real destination—the spiritual one. The material world, with all its miseries, makes us fail to think about and prepare for the eternal kingdom. We get sucked-in by vanity, bitterness, envy, anger, and too much enjoyment; we think we have arrived and get too comfortable. With God, it's not really a long-distance relationship, because he's omnipresent. That's why, with any shake-up, however little we call to him—oh, my God.

CHAPTER 48

Oh, my God, how nice that you give one an opportunity to reflect on sweet life with its trials and challenges. Oh, my God, that sometimes we can be so wicked and don't count our blessings, evaluating our relationship with you by listing our misfortunes, some of them well earned through our own unrighteousness. Oh, my God, that you have not kept a record of my wrongs and found me unworthy of your love, that has kept me going even at the hardest of times, that you have given me your grace and favour to make a difference in many people's lives and to receive the same from those that have touched my life. That some can now share my own life's experiences and know me better.

There are other wars besides the shooting ones, but if they have to be fought, the parties have to be brave, prepared and not to waver. In life, many things look like contradictions, and yet they are mutually dependent. Some crises are of our own making, and some of our own words could be potentially damaging, but there's so much goodness in life, and good people out there. We only need to master the one important skill of communicating and persuading. Then we will find that we do not need much magic but if we make no effort, we might also lose the moment. Nothing is too hard to try.

CHAPTER 49

My sister Kate is much younger than I am, and she exudes a lot of energy. She has taken on so much of what I used to do, especially within the family, and much more. I cannot claim she learnt some of that from me, if she did, then she has excelled beyond what I could ever have done. The student has surpassed the teacher. I had always been there for all in the family, in joy and in sorrow. Now I am not near because of work, but Kate is fantastic support to all of us. I do not mean to imply that everyone else is not responsible, but shouldn't exceptions be mentioned? I at one time or another lived with most of my sisters—Lillian, Kate, and Lucy more than the rest, and Florence not so much in my house, but now her house is home for Eva and Joshua in England. That's what family in the true African sense is. On my mother's side, I have looked after and lived with Jacinta, but Stella one of the twins who followed me, has been outstanding in my life. I can share anything without fear of being misunderstood. I do not have to rehearse my words, because Stella and I click naturally. She knows how badly I longed to bond with my mother, from whom I was separated at an early age, and I had not got the chance until a month ago when I brought her to visit with me in Arusha, Tanzania. She stayed for about four weeks. I now appreciate how much of my mother I had not know, how harshly I had judged her, how deep a mother's bond can be, and more importantly, how different we all are however much we may want to be the same.

I lived with my brother Godfrey, who followed the twins, but he, too, has grown to be remote and distant, which does not make him bad, really; I guess it's his way of coping with his own family life. I love my sisters-in-law, but I also need to be mindful of their space and respect their husbands in a way different from what I knew them to be—my kid brothers. If you do not apply that love appropriately, you may not know you are all over someone like a bad rash and you may mistake little courtesies for rights. I in particular know better than to invade people's space or take anything for granted, so I offer as much as I can and take only what I think I have been given. With family, I avoid acting rashly or with emotional impulses to minimize regret, but even when my expectations are not met, I try not to live in the past. We move on, while I try always to ensure that I will be the guide to life for many, lighting the path ahead to be followed by others, a place naturally given to me by God, as the first child of both my parents, followed in total by sixteen siblings.

CHAPTER 50

Public expression of love is an individual choice that does not particularly fly with me, maybe because I am conservative. It does not—in my view—necessarily reflect the depth. It's just a convenient way of making a statement, not to yourself or even the person you love, but to the world, that yours is a soap opera and your wish is that it overwhelms whoever sees it, even if it does not overwhelm you. Sometimes the artificiality of such expressions offend other people, and you cannot say to me it's none of their business; otherwise, why do you want them to see? I am a strong believer that affairs are private matters. I differ from those who think if you're in love and happy, it should be shouted from the roof tops. I said earlier that there's no universal definition of what love is or is not, similarly I doubt there should be a common standard on how to express it, mine is just a personal opinion, which might even sound archaic and outdated, but I think I am entitled to it, just as everyone else is entitled to theirs. Whenever people are too loud, it's an involuntary, subconscious pretence of confidence, an overcompensating defence mechanism. When it comes to matters such as this one, I need to find the right balance between telling my story and telling it accurately without compromising other people's privacy and comfort. The shortcomings of my marriage and the eventual resolution did not impose a permanent scar on my emotional being. There was a wound, all right, to my emotional being, and to my part in a society that still views those vows I took as a life sentence. Recently, one friend with a stubbornly high sense of humour proposed an amendment to marriage vows: 'For better I stay, for worse I go.' If you want to take such honest and more practical vows, then the church is not your place to go for a wedding. In fact the church has unrealistically refused to accept divorces, even when they are provided for in the church constitution—the Bible. But I also know as a good Christian that the Bible is one of the most controversial books ever written. It contains many contradictions, so much so that an aspect of, or a scenario in, the Bible could be interpreted to have two extremely opposite meanings.

When people rush to church to be joined in Holy Matrimony, I have yet to hear any who rush back when they want out. Whenever I look at my divorce certificate, issued by a legitimate court of law, alongside the marriage one, issued by another legitimate social institution, I wonder how the former could nullify the latter. Fortunately, church is not legally mandated to try cases—whether civil or criminal. So, conveniently, a social and emotional matter gone sour becomes a legal issue, or more precisely a human-rights one.

I was mindful not to jump into relationships, especially in the immediate aftermath of my separation and eventual divorce. I had to tread very carefully, because I had a legal process to deal with to free myself from a union I had consciously and willingly entered into and was likewise ready to abandon. Any wrong move and I would have been the guilty party, of adultery if it could be proved, desertion, name it. I was also still going through a kind of emotional healing, but I was determined to take charge of the situation and not let the situation take charge of me. I had to be level-headed and focused, with a clear view of where exactly I wanted to go. I had two young children to look after, and I was determined to give them my all. Their father had not thought about them in all that had happened between us, and I was not going to behave in the same way. They needed stability and I was the one to give it to them. My own life and emotional needs had to be suppressed, at least for a while. I had to consciously choose the right people to associate with at the right time and in the right places. It's like choosing the appropriate dress for every occasion. It requires one to be deliberate and conscious. Affairs had to have perimeters within which to operate, and I was too scared to commit, actually always ready to run whenever I thought someone wanted to cross the boundaries I had mentally drawn. With time, the human in us overpowers us, and though we can try to control it, we cannot live that lie forever. One trait I knew about myself over time, however, was that I could not elevate a relationship into more than it was. In actual fact, I found it better to underplay it whenever one developed. Better safe than sorry. Much as I preferred privacy, I hated being extremely clandestine, which again was unavoidable depending on the person I was associating with.

But that feeling of a joyous something looking shameful and wrong really waters down the whole thing so much, and with time it's bound to lose its taste and become sort of flat and boring. A woman of independent means also has a void to be filled—not necessarily shoes. It is interesting, though, when you can involuntarily exude the confidence that you are a woman with options. Don't read too much into this lest you miss the real point.

I had to let my hair down at some point, keeping within the limits of the parameters I had set for myself. Some of my relationships have been more serious than others, but another principle I keep is no casual sex, no multiple affairs—both have their own shortcomings and problems. I also have not had bad endings, so I have remained on friendly and civil terms with the few male friends I have been intimate with. I am told it's not very easy to get close to me, but once people do, it's very had not to be attached when I let them. I enjoy the trust and confidence such friends maintain with me, sometimes to the discomfort of someone else, but again, one thing I don't do is go back. My life moves always forward—to the future, not the past. By the time you stop an affair, it is important to be convinced that you're doing the right thing and that it's exactly what you want. You should not threaten to quit when actually you don't mean it. It can be counterproductive. One former boyfriend of mine whom I met when he was going through a divorce had not got it then; years later he simply became a victim of this emotional trick. But his was not simply an affair, it was a marriage—so the change of mind was cushioned by some protection. Four years after we met, he still believed he was divorcing 'soon' and marrying me. He shared with me the contents of his court file whenever there was a new development, until it was clear that when his wife proposed divorce, she actually did not mean it. I think she simply meant to make him aware of some things that did not please her, to attract more attention and be offered more love. He got it all wrong and instead acted naively or arrogantly and accepted the divorce, thereby hurting her feelings and her pride. She could have tried to find love the wrong way, but being a solicitor, she acted first and smartly, at the cost of looking ridiculous—she made it difficult. I, funnily enough, found myself counselling him that what she had wanted was for him to beg, promise more love, apologize, and repent if he'd wronged her, but not to readily agree to the divorce and go ahead with getting another woman in preparation. He's an African American living in England and certainly aware of the legal implications if he pushes it. It was not until she asked for 70 per cent of his present assets and 50 per cent of any future income that he woke up. I had already woken up when my name once came up during the legal proceedings. I had had my share of divorce proceedings; I did not need to share anyone else's. Whether they will live happily after dropping the case that had gone on for six years is the least of my concerns, but it is a lesson many should learn. As for me, I moved on, fast and forward. When I am moving, as a principle, I look ahead, not behind.

CHAPTER 51

Moving on does not necessarily mean moving to better places. Just keep moving. You might stumble and sometimes fall, but for God's sake get up and move. As you move, you will meet people—bad people, good people, friends, lovers, or soul mates (a title not reserved for everyone that you joke with, dine and wine with, dance with, or even go to bed with). In a lifetime, very few will serve you to your satisfaction—total unswerving commitment, reliance, and trust.

The people in my 'inner circle' know the blissful happiness I have enjoyed for some years now because of the one special person who loves me dearly and to whom my heart has unreservedly opened. I do not want to sound dramatic, but it's a nice feeling to be loved for what you are and to enjoy each minute you spend with someone without feeling like you are making a sacrifice. We feel very good together. I particularly enjoy his high sense of humour, his wide knowledge and experience, the love and trust, telling things without having to rehearse them, laughing from the heart, and sharing any fears and anxieties. This shouldn't sound like a convenient fairy tale, but 'happy' and 'happiest' are two different feelings, so if you want to be accurate, it's important to make a distinction.

If someone offers him or herself, it is different from offering material things. In your own calculation, you can distinguish between love, obsession, and infatuation. You should also make a deliberate decision what you want to take, to keep, to throw away, or to ignore. Having enough money to make my life comfortable, considerable fame to maintain a sane life, two good children, and a number of friends, I don't want to hassle so much with life, asking for too much, and this love crowns it all. My favourite verse from 'Clothes of Heaven' by William Butler Yeats goes:

Had I the heavens' embroidered cloths,
Enwrought with golden and silver light,
The blue and the dim and the dark cloths
Of night and light and the half light,
I would spread the cloths under your feet:
But I, being poor, have only my dreams;
I have spread my dreams under your feet.
Tread softly because you tread on my dreams.

It is such a nice feeling to think like this about somebody, but he brings stability into my life, so I may as well.

Life is nice when it is simpler and ordinary, accepting that there's something different from one person to another, choosing whom to allow in your life, avoiding being pushed into intolerable situations from which sometimes there's no way back. A small centimetre of understanding, friendship, and support can make a great change, while likewise an error of judgement, or an outright careless mistake, can sabotage a beautiful friendship. You can choose to deal with people who are not emotionally and spiritually stunted. From a crowd, you may not easily identify the people you need—genuine, simple, down-to-earth, and sincere. Maybe sometimes you decide to choose what is avoidable: the middle-of-the-road, a bit naïve, not so detailed, a bit sincere, and not necessarily honest. The packages are not always that clear-cut, but you also need self-assessment, and the courage to turn yourself inside-out, the mental housecleaning to be taken seriously. Sometimes if you concentrate on the positives, and they by far outweigh the negatives, then you don't get saddled with what would otherwise be barriers in life. You can also turn those few negatives into positives, as I have done to package a life of a smooth childhood, lots of love from parents, grannies, steps, uncles, aunties, siblings, friends, and later in life, children. I spice it up with having been an above-average student, physically not so bad, with an interesting career. When I want to do a self-appraisal, then I go to things like my personality—strong but also considerate of others, attending to details but not trivial—and then I realize I am making excuses for myself when I start the buts, and finally decide that a little gossip and laughter could add a sparkle to an otherwise dull and too serious lifestyle.

The silence of my present home has had a calming effect on me, sometimes getting me frightened that I might forget to laugh and be warm to people, and then I quickly remember that I am one person who has no emotional baggage or dependency syndrome to make me sad. Without thinking about it, I act like a woman, spontaneously, because I am one, and a mother of two who gives constant love and attention, providing security and confidence to all those I love, emphasizing to them responsibility, forgiveness, and other values. For the children, I never stop talking about self-preservation, especially in light of what is happening with youngsters lately; sustainability, when their appetites for extravagance get higher than I can tolerate; consistency, when I notice any traces of twisted facts; and simplicity and modesty, when peer pressure seems to be taking a toll on my pocket. Sometimes when as I am talking very seriously, I see them exchanging glances, probably restraining themselves from bursting into laughter. I've not overheard them, but I suspect after the lectures, they laugh and maybe do not call me names but probably come to a conclusion like Mum must be suffering from mid-life crisis. I, however, believe that they more often pick what I am saying, especially 'self-analysis' and 'self-evaluation'. It is important every so often for one to have time and space to refocus and take stock.

CHAPTER 52

When taking stock, sometimes your mind can wander to areas that you may not influence directly, but which catch the eye and mind whether one wants or not. Having been in politics, I regularly and instinctively wander back. Being an economist and public policy graduate at Harvard's Kennedy School of Government, I cannot avoid re-examining political and economic reforms and wondering how effective they have been or if they are long overdue to be reviewed. I often wonder how much I should keep quiet, without feeling guilty of a conspiracy of silence if there is something I feel should be done differently. But also I realize that sometimes I do not have a platform to air my development and employment creation views, and my advocacy for the role of government as an engine of growth without compromising the general principal of free enterprise, and probably the importance of governance issues in economic development. I have lately decided to write short articles for the newspapers, hoping that one or two policy makers might find something useful and pick it. I have had to be very careful not to over-criticize, even when I am dying to, aware that if your idea is to be looked at twice, it should from the start be seen to be politically correct. Sometimes I wish we could sit in round-table discussions, call them think tanks if you want, but there should be an avenue to agree on how to steer our countries in a manner that is strategic, with policies that are holistic and approaches that are integrated. How I wish, on issues of social welfare, we could read from the same page. Sometimes when you think you are on the same page, you realize it was different books and you're therefore going in different directions. I have decided, however, that it's not a total waste of time to keep trying. So whenever I meet people who are not bored by discussions about economic development, social transformation, or even good governance and accountability, I engage them until they change the topic. It's amazing how many people in leadership indulge in rhetoric without necessarily walking the walk.

When refocusing and taking stock of where, for example, my country Uganda has come from, where it is, and where it should be going, I made one judgement—it's personal, so no one will go to jail for it—that my President Yoweri Museveni missed the opportunity to implement his transformational ambitions as well as he had intended, and that nothing now can change things drastically. It is not a treasonable thought, and realists should take it seriously. Those that are in the position to should propose a return to the drawing board. When the freedom fighter got caught in the web of modern politics, in a society that had suffered decadence and understood more the language of decisions by order and force, it was hard to get the right balance. People quickly forgot that authority is to be both feared and respected. The leader allowed himself to be dragged into small issues, by small people as well as big ones. Almost any group of people—bus owners, clearing agents, rental motorcyclists, traditional leaders and healers, name it—has had easy access to the president through their vigilant parliamentary representatives, ministers, or group leaders, who know someone who knows someone who is related to someone who works somewhere with easy access.

The president has had to deal with so many interest groups, sometimes making contradictory promises, often to the disappointment of his appointed policy makers. The beginning was well intentioned, broad-based reform. But because it was handled badly, or prolonged beyond its right time, things got out of hand. There should have been a set limit to the honeymoon; personally, I think it should have ended in 1996 when President Museveni won his first democratic elections. He then had the opportunity to select a winning team and rid himself of political excess baggage, people he had recruited into the ranks of his government not because of their qualification, competences, loyalty, or even experience, but because they belonged to this or that former fighting group. The criteria continued to disaggregate, to cater to the balancing of regions, tribes, gender, or religion without due regard to quality. I keep joking that soon there may be a balancing of the tall and the short, the light- and the dark-coloured. This could also be part of the reason for micro management people have been given work they are not capable of doing. In the end, you are over-stretched, overworked, and subconsciously undermining your own incremental approach with each inch promptly reversed by several feet as you move from one project to another, managing crisis after crisis. Follow-up, when implementers have not been part of the decision or design, is not easy. The vision is not shared, what would be successful stories are like dripping water on a stone because they are met with hardness and sometimes indifference. In the middle of all this, there is the hard fact that Uganda has to deal with corruption, obscurantism, pure ignorance, and selfishness. Decisions take forever to be implemented, if at all, because they are not followed through to their logical conclusions. The big man gets frustrated and thinks that no one can deliver except him. I keep hoping that sometimes he sees through the lies his lieutenants feed him, even when there is no light at the end of the tunnel. Sometimes I am not even sure he thinks there is a problem. I might be wrong, and I pray I am, so that when he gets power again in two years' time he chooses a winning team, not to win elections but to wind up Uganda's transition to the long-awaited fundamental change.

CHAPTER 53

The fundamental change is again what we need to make East Africa more competitive, stable, and politically united, as its vision goes. With two years to go as a Deputy Secretary General in charge of fast-tracking the process towards East African political federation, each activity I embark on with my team is one step towards that ultimate goal. I am a strong optimist that with the foundation we're attempting to lay, full integration will be only a matter of time. The countries agree in principle; some have a different view on the speed with which it should be implemented, but it is more on form than content. After all, the end justifies the means. We should distinguish between goals and by-products. I have endeavoured to make the message loud and clear. It is impossible to claim not to have heard it. We had better integrate or perish. But we should as a matter of necessity address basic governance issues.

What we have not managed to achieve singularly, I am very confident we can collectively, because it is easier to coordinate one planning unit than several sovereign ones. In a bigger unit, the interests to please are subsumed and minimized, so we can attend to bigger issues of development by thinking big. These are not contradictory but mutually dependent. On integration, I keep watching and wishing that countries and their leaders will not only make more responsible decisions but also commit to implementing them. We cannot afford—and the time is up—to continue blaming someone else for our woes. A problem is better looked at as it is, not how it started. Instead of concentrating on how to heal the pain, we have spent more on who caused it, living in the past. It is true that Africa's balkanization was a political, resource-driven jigsaw puzzle of weird configurations with no physical barriers. All physical infrastructure was designed to transport goods—raw materials—to Europe, with no inter-linkage within Africa. The containment policy denied some countries access to the sea. But Africans have gone beyond blaming others for the problem, and instead owned it. The North/South divide in some countries or West/East in others because of different religions or colour shade is a clear and living example. African countries have accepted tokenism through donations from the parts of the world that systematically manipulated us, now conveniently baptized 'developed partners'. I don't hate them. In fact, I have many friends out there. I have studied with them and certainly enjoy the new language they have introduced, enriching our vocabulary tremendously. I cannot find perfect substitutes and do not know how we would explain certain things if they had not invented phrases like bottom-up, stakeholder participation, Millennium Development Goals (MDGs), Poverty Reduction Strategy Papers (PRSPs), decentralization, private-sector-led economies, benchmarking and, lately, ring-fencing. The process of the EAC integration and eventual federation is one I am happy and proud to have participated in. It is an issue that should remain at the top of our concerns. I am not bothered that there have been arrogant remarks in the past that could potentially undermine the integration process, but I am bothered by repeated attempts to explain and justify them. East Africa should not lose the moment. It should be part of a reformed integral global order with a deliberate and systematic developed agenda.

CHAPTER 54

Is it possible that we can save our societies from extreme hopelessness caused by desperation? Desperation in turn has its roots in the rampant, extreme poverty, and loss of hope and of faith in what the world has to offer. This has created, among other things, groups of fundamentalists—whether religious or otherwise. What does society do with someone not scared of taking his or her own life? The one month I spent in Afghanistan in 2004 as a Consultant for USAID was one nightmare I'll never forget. I was contracted to carry out training in parliamentary procedures for the first ever elected parliament in Afghanistan. As a woman, non-Muslim, English speaking, I had to 'do as the Romans do'—cover my head, wear long, mostly black dresses, and take it all in without expressing shock openly. In the middle of a lecture, if it was time, I would hear one person start: *Allah Akbar*—and the chorus would begin, women would have to leave and go to another room and I would stand there stupidly until I also slowly went outside until prayer time was over. What was more serious, however, was experiencing the life of terror when, in a car, I looked back and saw the vehicle behind mine go up in flames. When I could not know where the next grenade would be detonated—by someone willing to take people's lives and his along with them.

I have taken time to understand the extra dimension to the fear factor. The psychology of a suicide bomber succeeds in making a population live in fear; it effortlessly wields a murder weapon. And the fact that in some countries, it could be that person standing next to you as you enter a place of prayer, wait to board a bus or train, board a plane, or even carry a baby to see a doctor. People who have lost faith on life on earth and hope to enjoy some fruits of the afterlife. Somehow I feel confident that the youth in our society, however unemployed and suffering, would rather have their rewards here and now. They will get what they want through means that will hurt us, unless we pay more attention to them. In East Africa, young men or women may not strap bombs around their midriffs and detonate them, but left alone, they can lob grenades from a safe distance, killing others but keeping themselves alive. The harm will nevertheless be done. These people are not necessarily sadists or mentally deranged; they are able-bodied, strong young people, with no work, no income, and no hope.

Governments therefore have the great challenge to direct public policy towards employment creation. Vocational training to foster self-employment, and investment in science and technology cannot be avoided, and this is a primary responsibility of governments. Governments cannot run away from their role as an engine of growth. The private sector can propel the economy, but its motive is profit, and it will not invest in the public good; it's not the private sector's cardinal duty.

CHAPTER 55

In *Making a Difference* I have touched on many aspects of life and tried to package them in a simple, and I hope interesting, manner. Nothing academic, nothing so serious. What I can only promise is to write a better book next time and to do it faster so that issues are not overtaken by events.

Reading this book, you may like some things and not others, you may not necessarily agree with everything. These are my personal experiences, thoughts, fears, successes, and failures. If I have not displayed elegance and sophistication, do not get disappointed, for that was not my intention. A difference is not made by big or complicated things. Sometimes what you see is not what you get and books do not always necessarily match their covers. That is the mystery of reality—that for every corner you turn, there is something different from the previous one. For every episode in your life, the experience is different, even if only marginally. From the people you meet, there's something new to learn; even if you do not emulate it, keep it in your mind. You never know when you may need to apply it. You may not always hear what you want, but some things are hard to ignore.

If you light a candle and keep it under the bed, think again whether you should have lit it at all. You cannot afford to let rot what you cherish, because once something is rotten, it cannot be good again.

Getting to know other people's difficulties may make you feel better, for in this world there are always worse-off people, but there are also better people. My final advice: Smile. God loves you.

Strive to make a difference, however small. Collectively and incrementally, our actions, if well targeted, should make this world a better place to live in.